DIGITAL TOUCH POINTS
How to Gain a Competitive Advantage Using Video and Dynamic Media

Practical Tips for Executives

Randy Palubiak

Copyright © 2013 Randy Palubiak

All rights reserved. No part of this book may be reproduced, stored in a retrieval system or transmitted in any form or by any means, electronic, mechanical, photocopying, recording or otherwise, without the prior written permission of the author or Enliten Management Group, Inc.

While every precaution has been taken in the research and compilation of this book, the accuracy of the information contained herein cannot be guaranteed and the author makes no representations or warranties, whether expressed or implied, as to the accuracies of the information contained herein.

Printed in the United States of America

ISBN 978-0-9895548-0-0

Enliten Management Group, Inc.
www.enliten.net
Atlanta, GA

Dedicated to

Diane, Courtney, Chandra, Corey, Shelby and Cayden

Acknowledgements

I want to acknowledge the organizations that allowed me the opportunity to assist with their video and media-based challenges. Without them, there would be no foundation for this book.

Special thanks to those individuals who provided insight and guidance to make this book an informative and effective tool for corporate executives. Most notably: David Lamb, Marvin Mitchell, Bill Marriott, Craig Palubiak, Rick Darby and Dr. Jolly Holden.

Purpose

This book is designed to provide business executives vision, structure and guidance for gaining a competitive advantage via the use of video and dynamic media.

It provides executives a perspective on how digital media is impacting the enterprise space and how many companies are using technology and different media channels.

It provides practical tips and recommendations on how to leverage existing and emerging technology and methods to create enormous business value for the company.

Contents

Foreword	xi
Executive Overview	xii
Introduction	xiii

Chapter 1

Video as a Strategic Communications Tool	1
The Power of Video – Winning Elections	1
Video's Valued Role in the Enterprise	2
Key Drivers and Benefits of Video and Dynamic Media	5

Chapter 2

Digital Touch Points	9
Reach and Empower Customers and Employees	9
Reaching Everyone, Everywhere, on Multiple Screens	11
The Empowered Viewer!	12
Blurred Lines Brings Clarity and Opportunity	14

Chapter 3

Content is King	19
It's All About the Content – Content is Still King!	19
Relevant Content and Information	20
Is it Live or On-Demand	25
Right Amount of Relevant Content	26
Customers / Consumers Want Content	28
If the Content is Applicable, Use It Time and Time Again	29
Whence it Comes? The Conundrum!	30

Chapter 4

Establish a Media Business Strategy	35
Incorporate Media Strategies into Business Plan	35
Implement the Media Channels	36
As TV and Computers Have Converged	37

Get Everyone on the Same Page	38
Communication, Training and Marketing Requirements	41
Video is Just Another Application:	41
Video Ecosystem is Robust and Flourishing	42
Look to Media-centric Providers	43
Governance – Protect the Brand and Video Workflow	43
The Business Model	44

Chapter 5

Viewing Locations and Environments	**47**
Viewing Locations: Reach Them Where it Counts!	47
On-Premise Group, Public or Individual Settings	48
Communicate to All Employees, Not Just Most	50

Chapter 6

Blend Digital Media Channels	**53**
Leverage Channels and Resources to Maximize ROI	53
Cross-Functional Collaboration	54
The Video Ecosystem: A Robust, Flexible Business Tool	57
Implement a Hybrid Content Delivery Network	60
Business Television (BTV) and Video Networks	62
Public Internet and Corporate Channels	66
Digital Signage	70
Mobile Devices	75
Surveillance Systems	77
The Cloud – Cloud Services	78
Staffing Resources Go Media-Centric!	81
Business Drivers of Blended Communications	82

Chapter 7

Analytics	**85**
Striving for Business Intelligence: Results!	85
Analytics	86
Learning and Training	87

Chapter 8
Protect Company Media Assets   **91**

   Digital Workflow – DAMs & MAMs   91

   Metadata   94

   Benefits and Business Drivers: 97

   Historical Value   98

   Managing Video and Dynamic Media Assets   99

   Consequences of Maintaining Status Quo?   100

Chapter 9
Managed Video as a Service (MVaaS)   **105**

   MVaaS vs. Home-grown   107

   Managed Staffing Resources as a Service   108

   Role of the Vendor   109

   Service Level Agreements & Key Performance Indicators   110

   Business Drivers and Key Benefits   111

Summary   **115**

   Roadmap to Success   115

Resources   **117**

Foreword

New media technology and applications are evolving at a rapid pace. How consumers and employees use the technology to view video and rich media content is changing just as fast.

Companies are challenged with keeping up, but face numerous questions and issues to address such as:

- What media to embrace?
- How to address the constant influx of new media?
- How to leverage the Cloud?
- How to manage the video and rich media content?

Although the tools are changing, the mission and objectives of companies using the media remain constant: increase sales and improve customer satisfaction.

Executives must assess their specific situations and set the best direction for their companies. They should develop a media business strategy to clearly define who the company is trying to reach, when and where and a build a communication plan that addresses how best to use video and dynamic media.

Now is the time to get everyone in the organization on the same page and leverage the company's existing systems and infrastructure with the right blend of new technology and media channels.

Executive Overview

Gaining Competitive Advantage via Video and Dynamic Media Strategy

Why video and dynamic media?

The effective use of video and dynamic media can substantially improve communications, marketing and training in your company: Increasing revenues, decreasing and/or off-setting costs, and improving your customers' experience and satisfaction.

> "Customer experience is how your customers perceive their interactions with your company."[1]

They can be competitive differentiators for your company!

Why now?

The tools and uses of video and dynamic media are available, with more entering the market every day.

Consumers are embracing them with both zest and zeal:

> *Invigorating excitement* and *enthusiastic devotion*.

Although the technology can be challenging and implementation and utilization overwhelming, companies are starting to get their hands around it. Get there first!

Why this book?

It will provide you, your staff, and other stakeholders throughout the company a common understanding of a media business strategy, the Cloud, asset management and analytics. Get everyone to the table and it will help get them on the same page.

It will provide a framework to start the process of gaining a competitive advantage with video and dynamic media.

---

[1] Manning, Harley and Bodine, Kerry; (2012). *Outside In: The Power of Putting Customers at the Center of Your Business*, Amazon (2012).

Introduction

We are in a "video, dynamic media and mobile-centric society" with an abundance of devices and applications to inform, influence, entertain, and educate individuals at home, away from home and in the work place.

As new media technologies have evolved and their applications increased, people have embraced these communication tools to meet their individual interests and needs. Quite often, they are multi-tasking on various devices and leveraging the strengths and abilities of each device to enhance their user experience.

Essentially, we have cut the cords that once bound us to personal computers and televisions and are now enjoying the freedom of mobility: wireless, un-tethered communications for the consumption of content anytime, everywhere and on a variety of viewing devices.

The term "viewing on all four screens" has been coined, which refers to televisions, desktop monitors, laptops and tablets and smartphones. As the screen size decreases mobility increases. Wearable devices such as Google Glass and smartwatches may be embraced as the fifth screens.

> "People are going to do different things in different ways... The key is to understand that people are going to want various form factors, and they're going to not want to compromise on the amount of power they have, whether it's in their pocket for certain purposes, or at their desk for others."[2]
>
> Steve Ballmer, Microsoft CEO

Companies and other enterprise organizations such as government agencies and departments, associations and educational institutions, are aggressively striving to identify how to address the continuous introduction of new devices and the demands by their targeted audiences to view content when,

---

[2] *USA Today* January 2011.

where and how they want to consume it. The objective is for companies to use video and dynamic media to support and enhance their strategic business objectives.

> **Dynamic Media** is constantly changing and is interactive.
>
> Think: Social Media.
>
> **Video** is Media and can be dynamic.
>
> Think: Live Streaming; Videoconferencing - Telepresence; Digital Signage; Live Interactive Distance Learning; and Interactive Video-on-Demand.
>
> **Video can be very effective over Social Media.**

Successful companies are developing media business strategies to leverage video and dynamic media to improve brand awareness and business results by engaging customers and employees through an increase in *digital touch points.*[3]

> A **Digital Touch Point** is the reaching of an individual through an electronic device. More specifically, it is a point of contact when a person or a company provides a targeted customer or employee with information or content via a digital media channel for consumption on a digital device such as a television, computer screen, tablet, smartphone or other smart device.

The book will cover:

1. Video as a Strategic Communication Tool

---

[3] Palubiak, Randy, *Digital Touch Points: Reaching your audience on all four screens,* Hughes Network Systems (2012).

Dynamic communications and learning approaches are moving people to constantly participate, interact, share and collaborate.

2. **Digital Touch Points**

   Reach and empower customers and employees.

   Individuals expect to be as interactive at work as they are in their personal lives. They have become media-centric. Your company needs to be equally media-centric.

   Reach your customers and employees regardless of their media delivery preferences.

3. **Content is King**

   Do not let technology drive solution selections.

   Solution selection should be directed by how it can best meet your business, marketing, communications and training needs.

4. **Establish a Media Business Strategy**

   It should be inclusive of all departments and business units and leveraged across all media channels throughout the organization.

   Executives, marketing, sales and training and learning groups all have compelling needs to communicate.

5. **Viewing Locations and Environments**

   Consumers use devices of their preference to view and interact with video content when, where and how they choose. It is all about a good, engaging experience.

   Employees expect the same or greater capabilities in the work environment.

   Produce content for viewing on each appropriate screen.

6. **Blend Digital Media Channels**

   Companies are striving to reach their internal and external audiences while the media channels, viewing devices and other tools used to increase and improve digital touch points to both audiences are overlapping.

   Converge and unify technology and resources across user and functional support groups.

7. **Analytics**

   Capture analytics for each functional area using video and dynamic media.

   Mine the data to ensure improved business results.

8. **Preserve Company Media Assets**

   Preserve and protect your company's media assets.

   Implement the digital asset management (DAM) system that offers the best digital workflow for your company.

9. **Managed Video as a Service (MVaaS)**

   Companies are embracing the concept of purchasing equipment, software and/or staffing services as managed services. As much as possible, put the responsibility of the purchase, ongoing support, system performance and future-proofing on the vendor(s).

Chapter 1
Video as a Strategic Communications Tool

The Power of Video – Winning Elections

The 1960 presidential election is long-recognized as a close, competitive campaign, where a young charismatic and photogenic Kennedy won, due in large part to his on-camera appearance and presentation style during the televised debates.

> In 1960, John F. Kennedy and Richard Nixon squared off in the first televised presidential debates in American history. The Kennedy-Nixon debates not only had a major impact on the election's outcome, but ushered in a new era in which crafting a public image and taking advantage of media exposure became essential ingredients of a successful political campaign. They also heralded the central role television has continued to play in the democratic process.[4]

In his 1962 book *Six Crises*, Nixon reflects on his role in a number of major political situations including the 1960 campaign, stating, *"I should have remembered that 'a picture is worth a thousand words.'"*[5]

The Internet became a powerful communications tool during the 2008 presidential election where the eventual winner, Barack Obama, effectively leveraged Facebook and social media. Obama supporters uploaded more than 1,800 videos, including the "Yes We Can" video by Will.i.am of Black Eyed Peas, to the YouTube *BarackObama.com* channel and attracted more than 97 million video views.

---

[4] *The Kennedy – Nixon Debates*, History.com
[5] Nixon, Richard M., *Six Crises*, Doubleday (1962).

Only 330 videos were posted to the YouTube channel for challenger John McCain and attracted about 25 million views.[6] In 2012, the Obama campaign leveraged the *techno-demographic appeal* he had established with social media and the extensive database of information it had compiled to "model behaviors and coordinate and target communications"[7] of prospective voters. However, the televised debates and on-line videos significantly contributed to President Obama's re-election. The video which may have had the most impact on the outcome was an unauthorized recording of opposing candidate Mitt Romney speaking at a fundraising event. In the video, he made the "47 percent" remark about the voters he felt certain would not vote for him. The video appeared on *motherjones.com* shortly before the election and immediately went viral.

Today, and going forward, elections will be contested primarily using video, including: commercials, news coverage, interviews, debates and video clips. The content will be broadcast or streamed live or downloaded for on-demand viewing. It will be intricately and extensively woven into the then popular social media channels.

Politicians are not the only ones who recognize the power and value of video. Executives in enterprise organizations of all sizes and types are embracing video more than ever.

Video's Valued Role in the Enterprise

Companies have embraced video communications since the 1950s when a number of corporations started using terrestrial telephone company circuits to distribute ad-hoc programs to hotel ballrooms and meeting rooms throughout the country. In the mid-1970's, ½" and ¾" videotape became viable media for enterprises replacing 35mm slides and 16mm film as the industry standard for presentations and sharing of information. Over the next couple of decades:

---

[6] Matthew Fraser and Soumitra Dutta, *Barack Obama and the Facebook Election* (USNews.com, November 2008).
[7] Dr. Pamela Rutledge, *How Obama Won the Social Media Battle in 2012 Presidential Campaign* (Media Psychology, January 2013).

- Hundreds of companies installed satellite-based business television and interactive distance learning networks;
- Thousands of companies implemented two-way videoconferencing systems, some of them with hundreds of communication units located in offices globally;
- Virtually every company used videotape;

...all to distribute video content, for a variety of applications including:

- Executive updates and communications;
- Town-hall meetings;
- Sales and marketing meetings and events;
- Employee and customer training;
- Current events, employee recognition programs;
- Product introductions;
- On-line marketing and merchandising; and
- Executive interviews with the news media and financial markets.

Today, we have advanced from traditional analog video to virtually everything digital: where we record digitally on video cameras, cell phones and even tablets; deliver content over digital media channels and systems; and view content on digital screens, which are getting larger and smaller.

We are to the point where consumer cameras record high quality, high definition (HD) pictures and video and commercially available software allows anyone to edit video on their personal computers. Also, the Internet, the Cloud, social media sites, satellite and terrestrial networks and a selection of hard media facilitate the delivery, exchange and limitless sharing of content.

More importantly, nearly everyone is producing video content: for personal consumption, to share with their social communities or at work in collaboration with their associates. Individuals, especially executives, have become more comfortable in front of the camera, whether being interviewed or performing as talent. Simply, more companies are using video, to conduct more communications, to a wider audience, more frequently, and with better quality.

> "...video will become the leading way people communicate."[8]

John Chambers, Cisco chairman and CEO

Bottom line, video has become today's essential means to communicate. It competes effectively with the phone, email and other traditional channels. The equipment and software solutions are affordable, feature robust capabilities and are easier to use.

According to David Lamb, principal of exec-U-tive and former Chief Learning Officer for numerous Fortune 500 companies,

> *"Workforce learning professionals have always had a bias for using video. However, the affordable cost of today's easy-to-use tools with increased power has ignited the use of video for training and performer support. This is truly a breakthrough in producing learning solutions with a very high return on investment."*

Statistics are published on a near daily basis on the increase in media usage and viewing. Here are some of the recent headlines, findings and projections:

33.5M US Mobile Users Watch Video

147M Americans Watch Video Online[9]

Digital Signage Deployments Growing

Digital Signage Sales to Grow to $13.2B by 2016[10]

---

[8] Cisco Live Conference (July 2011)
[9] Nielsen, *Internet and Mobile Video Audiences* (May 2012) Marketingcharts.com

Mobile Video Users Rise 43% Year-Over-Year

U.S. Online Video Use Up 45 Percent, Year-Over-Year[11]

Executive Use of Business Video Is Already Mainstream
....79% of business executives use two-way business video at least once a week

Online Video Increases eCommerce Conversions 30 Percent

Video in the C-Suite: Executives Embrace the Non-Text Web

Online video will make up 91 percent of consumer IP traffic

If the statistics and pundits are correct, and it is they likely are, it is critical that you get ahead of the curve and exploit video to give your organization a competitive advantage.

As the use of video increases, companies will embrace and adapt to a variety of media channels. Video will be produced on multiple platforms and delivered at various bandwidth rates.

Key Drivers and Benefits of Video and Dynamic Media

Key business drivers and benefits for using video and dynamic media in the enterprise may include:

- Enhanced brand;
- Increased sales;
- Improved efficiencies in employee productivity;

---

[10] Matt Pillar, *Capture Online Sales with Digital Signage*, Integrated Solutions for Retailers (February 2013)

[11] *U.S. Online Video Use Up 45 Percent, Year-Over-Year* (2011) Clickz.com

Digital Touch Points

- Improved customer service, by providing timely and consistent information;
- Reduced costs by leveraging existing facilities, tools and resources;
- Reduced employee turnover;
- Higher retention than static information, e.g.: print, graphics, etc.;
- Improved timeliness of information creation and distribution.

Based on the value video and dynamic media can bring to a company, they have earned a place at the table.

Tips and Perspectives

- People are enamored with video:
  For information as well as sharing and collaboration.
- People will embrace various and different ways to receive and consume video content:
  On screens such as large television displays, computers, tablets and other mobile devices.
- Their obsession with new media will increase, changing and upgrading devices regularly:
  As they seek the best tools to enrich their viewing and interactive experience.
- There will always be new media and technology:
  An endless flow of new mousetraps.
- New media will be introduced or evolve at an ever-increasing pace:
  Video solutions are improving and expanding at computer-type speeds.
- Corporate communications, marketing and training requirements will grow and expand:

Due to the need to increase and improve customer and employee touch points, to address organizational right-sizing and generational differences, to respond to the fluctuating economy and globalization and to manage user and employee generated content.

- Executives will increase the use of video for live meetings and town hall events:
  Live, interactive engagement with employees and customers is invaluable.

- The demand for quality video will increase:
  Viewer expectations go higher as the quality of viewing devices improves;

  The quality of user-generated-content is not appropriate for every application.

- Video quality will be dynamically managed to the viewing device and environment suitable for the targeted audience.

- Organizations will preserve and protect their media assets:
  Historical and relevant content will be archived on asset management systems with robust search tools.

  Frequently viewed and re-purposed content may be located in-house and in the Cloud.

- Vendors and service providers will develop and implement effective, efficient solutions to meet their customers' requirements:
  They will enhance and expand existing systems and create or integrate other complementary solutions to increase and improve digital touch points and the user experience.

- Media and technologies for video use in companies have historically been derived from systems and solutions utilized in the consumer space, e.g.: video production, delivery, content management and display systems.
  This will continue.

  Follow trends set by broadcast networks, cable television and satellite providers; telecom, network and wireless providers; Internet service and content providers. Think DVR, high definition (HDTV) and ultra high definition (UHD), streaming, and video-on-demand (VoD). It will be an exciting ride.

It is not difficult to select media technologies and software solutions to address a specific requirement. However, it is challenging to select the right one(s) that effectively and efficiently work throughout the organization and interface and integrate with other technology and solutions.

To do it right requires the participation and buy-in of stakeholders from all departments and business units with a vested interest in digital touch points. It requires a collaborative, unified effort where an overarching business media strategy is absolutely critical!

Video and dynamic media have earned a place at the table.

Chapter 2
Digital Touch Points

Reach and Empower Customers and Employees

Over the past few years, we have experienced the convergence of video and data, the blending of media channels, the unifying of communication systems, and the increased use of collaboration tools. Basically, all of these technologies are coming together.

During this time, the use of video to educate, entertain, inform, and train has reached its highest levels ever. We have become a video and media-centric society. We have progressed to where we can be reached anywhere, anytime and on any viewing device.

Those in the advertising space might say, *it's all about the touch points* where the objective is to achieve a favorable CPM (cost per thousand views: impressions), and of course, sales results.

This chapter describes how enterprise organizations are delivering content using all types and forms of digital media to educate, inform and train: both customers and employees! The lines and digital touch points are clearly blending between where and how people access content and take action.

The following diagram shows the type of media in the ecosystem used to reach targeted internal and external audiences.

Digital Touch Points

Digital Touch Points
& the Enterprise Video / Dynamic Media Ecosystem

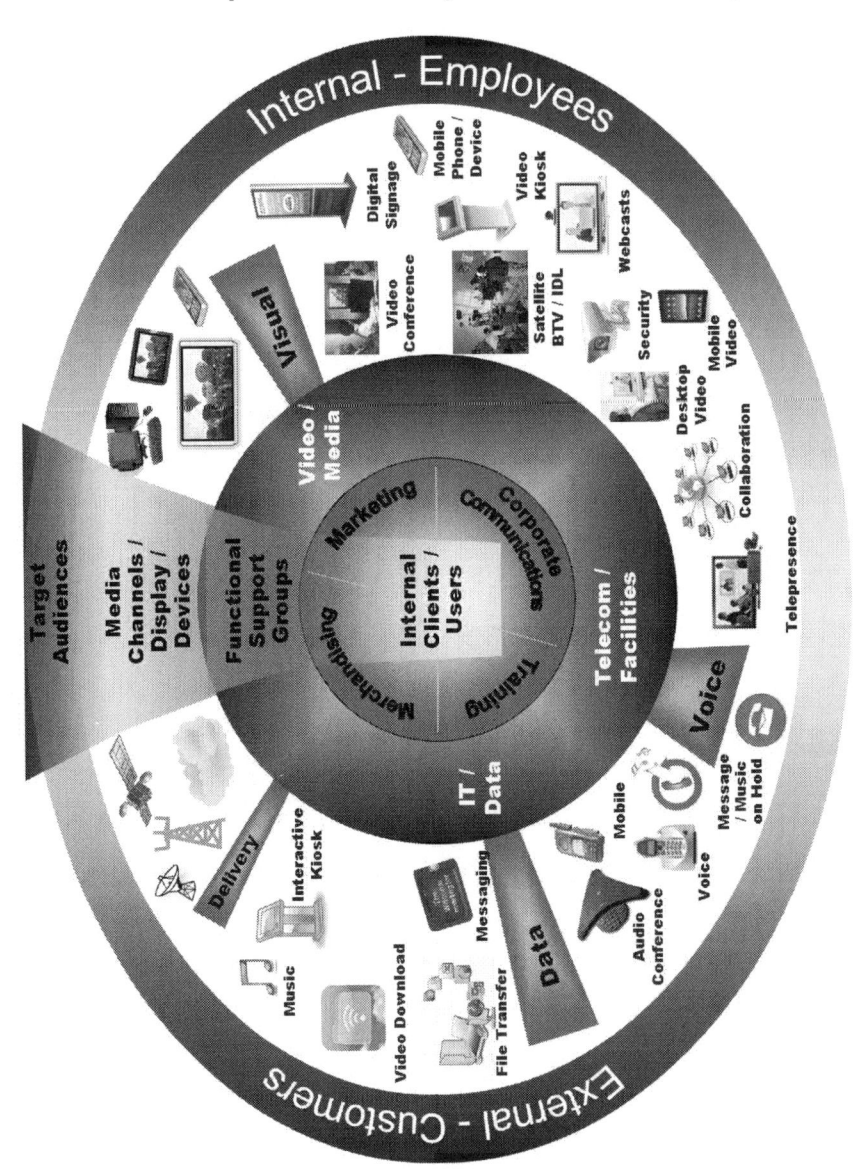

10

Digital Touch Points

Reaching Everyone, Everywhere, on Multiple Screens

Digital media channels and devices are what make touch points possible. As they are used to create, deliver, display and manage all of the content people and companies are producing. Briefly:

- Most everyone has created video content.
  It is so widely used that it has a name:
  User-generated content (UGC).
  In the enterprise, it is called:
  Employee-generated content (EGC).

- The content is distributed over a growing number of digital media channels, including but not limited to:
  - YouTube and other on-line video sites;
  - Personal, corporate and social media web-sites;
  - Emails and text messages as files or links;
  - Removable media such as flash drives and memory sticks.

- The content may be viewed:
  Live (in real-time) or at the convenience of the viewer (on-demand).

- The content may be displayed on:
  - Large screen televisions for:
    - Group meetings and sessions in break rooms, meeting rooms, training rooms, and conference rooms;
    - Digital signage applications in corporate lobbies and general traffic areas; in-store, showroom floor and other customer-facing areas; and outdoors.
  - Desktops for individual viewing;
  - Mobile devices such as laptops, tablets and smart phones.

You may be familiar with the term "viewing on all four screens." This refers to televisions, desktop screens, laptops, and tablets and phones. At some point, it may be changed to refer to "all five screens" to include wearable media. Whether it is four or five, these are screens most people use at both home and work and virtually everywhere in between.

In addition, interaction and feedback are critical components to successfully establishing digital touch points. Depending on the system design and viewing device, this may include audio interaction, responses via keypads and touch screens and the use of quick response (QR) codes.

Of course, implementing the media channels and establishing the number and type of desired digital touch points is only as good as the content and the means to measure its effectiveness. According to the Digital Place-based Advertising Association (DPAA)[12]:

> *"With the power of the right message, at the right time, at the right place you can leverage digital place-based media to either build awareness, increase purchase intent, activate mobile interaction or trigger a purchase right at the point of sale."*
>
> DPAA

The Empowered Viewer!
Viewers are No Longer Passive

There was a time when the major commercial networks (ABC, CBS and NBC), the Public Broadcasting Service (PBS) and local independent stations were responsible for providing all program content: no cable or pay-per-view channels. Our choices were limited, yet we were quite content to passively accept and select programs to view when the broadcasters elected to schedule them.

Jumping ahead to today, we the viewers have become empowered. We truly control the when, where and how we view commercial programming. In addition to broadcast television, cable and satellite television ensure that we have an abundance of content choices via a limitless number of channels. And now, Internet companies such as Netflix offer

---

[12] *What is Digital Place-based Media?* Dp-aa.org

original programming as well as the means to access other commercial and user-generated content (UGC). We have the power to view the content of our choice live or on-demand. Through the use of social media and personal devices, we are able to interact with programs and share the content and our thoughts with friends and other individuals within our communities of interest. In addition, we have the ability to create content (UGC) and the channels to distribute it (YouTube, Facebook, Twitter, etc.). Those who produce relevant content can actually build audiences like the commercial providers and attract sponsors and revenue sources. Consumers are truly empowered!

The Empowered Viewer

Passive	Select	Share	Produce
Watch Broadcast TV	Video-on-Demand	Community Services	Create Content

Rich Experience

One Service Fits All	Network Response	Personalize Socialize	Complete Customization
Broadcast	Transaction	Interaction	Empowerment

For better or worse, employees are similarly empowered. They use the same or similar display devices to view and consume content. They prefer short video clips to be informed and educated. They expect to have the ability to interact with the program sources and to share the content and their thoughts with others. Employees will accept the need to view some content live, but will typically prefer to view it at their convenience. They like to be in control.

Blurred Lines Brings Clarity and Opportunity
As Enterprises Reach both Internal and External Audiences

The lines are blurring between internal communications and training and external audiences for advertising, marketing, promotions and sales as the media channels and viewing devices continue to improve and be more ubiquitous.

As consumers modify their buying habits between on-line and in-store purchasing, advertising, marketing and promotions are conducted via digital media in-home, on-line, in-store and virtually everywhere on display screens of all sizes. Similar, if not the same, digital media are used to educate, inform and train employees. And now, employees are very likely using personal devices for business applications or vice-versa.

These and other contributing factors are very good for the enterprise community. Why? It creates opportunity for enterprises that recognize the value of video and digital media. The role and responsibility of the advertising community is to achieve a favorable CPM, using the best mix of media necessary. Those in enterprise communications should embrace a similar mindset. It is our role and responsibility to utilize the right blend of media solutions to effectively and efficiently reach target audiences: both external and internal digital touch points. It is equally important that the company have the right capabilities in place to drive individuals to action and then to evaluate and measure the results

The concept of empowerment applies to the use of mobile devices in the retail environment, where consumers use their smart phones and personal devices to search for information and items to purchase. While in-store, they use their devices to find information and pricing on desired items using QR codes, RFID (radio frequency identification) or other systems with a catchy acronym. Customers are bringing their on-line research and experience into stores: bringing "clicks" to "bricks." Retailers can enhance the customer experience by ensuring that sales associates are properly trained and have the tools to answer questions and provide additional or detailed information not readily available to the customer.

> Bringing "clicks" to "bricks."

Interactive displays and properly trained and equipped employees can obtain critical information through engagement with customers, about the customers, which can be invaluable to retailers. When combined with the analytics about customers acquired from their on-line shopping, retailers expand their knowledge of individual interests and buying tendencies.

In-store foot traffic and customer activity can be tracked and measured through the use of well-placed cameras. In many instances, this may include the same cameras and systems used for loss prevention applications. In addition, gaze technology systems can be used for facial recognition, where retailers can identify consumer demographics and be the basis for a wealth of marketing information.

These same capabilities and applications can be applied to any business or operation: they are not unique to retail. Digital displays and interactive systems can provide information and way-finding assistance throughout any building. Security cameras can provide analytics on foot traffic and activity in public and common areas without impacting their primary mission.

Many of the same systems used for internal applications can be used for external audiences, including: content creation systems, delivery infrastructure, display screens, interactive and measuring tools and content management systems. This can represent significant savings on capital expenditures, ongoing operation and maintenance, and staffing resources. It will be covered in more detail in Chapter 6: *Blend Digital Media Channels and Resources*.

Tips and Perspectives

Digital Touch Points

- Increase digital touch points:
  Utilize today's robust video and dynamic media solutions to expand your company's reach and increase the number of ways to communicate information and drive sales.

  The more visibility, the more opportunity for success!

- Empowered Viewers:
  Enable your targeted viewers to view and react to your company's message. Provide the tools and means to have customers take action at the register, prior to leaving the store.

  Allow, encourage and motivate viewers to engage with your company using the media device(s) with which they are the most comfortable. It will ensure an engaging experience for viewers and results for you.

- Performance Support:
  Give people access to video assistance (static or dynamic) at the time of need.

- Leverage your media channels to reach both internal and external audiences:
  Streamline the workflow and enjoy cost savings by implementing technology and software solutions to create, deliver and manage content to all target audiences.

  Extend the reach to all employees, regardless of location.

- Know your target audience(s):
  What are your employees saying?
  Are they expecting, demanding they be informed and trained differently?

- What are your customers saying?
  Are they responding favorably to video-based information and dynamic applications to interact with your corporate website and social media channels?

  Are they purchasing more products and services?

- Increase Revenues:

Improve and enhance the customer experience and motivate them to purchase more, by:

> *Providing information immediately, where and as they need it;*
>
> *Educating and training employees to knowledgeably assist customers;*
>
> *Collect and track customer interests and buying habits.*

Mine the analytics and consumer information to determine merchandising strategies and in-store product placements.

- Decrease and/or Manage Costs:
  Leverage the use of the same infrastructure and systems for both internal and external audiences: converge, merge and unify the effort and costs.

The savings may be significant.

Digital Touch Points

Chapter 3

Content is King

It's All About the Content – Content is Still King!

The single most critical piece to successful, profitable communications is content.

A company may have the most robust and extensive media channels possible. However, if it does not provide relevant and timely information, it might as well be screaming its message in a forest.

> *"...It's about the information, not the information technology."*[13]
>
> Peter Bloniarz, University of Albany, SUNY

Create the right message(s) to be delivered to the targeted audience(s). Then, focus on selecting the right delivery and display solutions to best address the specific and unique viewing environments. Do not be wowed by technology and the latest and greatest of flashy toys. This can be a costly and ineffective learning experience.

Technology selection will be addressed in other chapters including Chapter 4: *Establish a Media Business Strategy* and Chapter 6: *Blend Enterprise-wide Digital Media Channels.*

This chapter provides thoughts and perspectives on the different types of video content applications which can impact business results. The list has expanded in recent years as social media, technology and viewing devices have advanced. Key issues to address related to content include:

- Content must be relevant!
- Content should be easy to access, view and assimilate in a quick and timely manner.

---

[13] Peter Bloniarz, Dean of the College of Computing and Information at the University of Albany, State University of New York, *Atlanta Journal Constitution* (December 2008).

- Embrace the value and importance of live programs and messages!
- Understand the need for and value of on-demand programming.
- Use interactivity to encourage participation and drive engagement.
- Design the length of video programming according to the subject(s) and targeted audience(s).
- Provide the right amount of content:
    - Do not overwhelm employees with too much content.
    - Customers will demand more information and more information.
    - Be prepared to feed the beast!
- Use, re-purpose and re-use relevant content.

Relevant Content and Information

It is critical that content is relevant to the target audience and created correctly for presentation on each screen in the respective viewing environments. The content should be concise and easy to assimilate in a timely manner. This is no surprise. It is the formula embraced by companies which have used video over the past decades. During that period, a handful of applications have been the drivers for live corporate communications including:

- Company-wide town-hall meetings and executive messages;
- Motivation and cultural enhancement;
- Department and business unit meetings;
- Training classes and learning sessions;
- Public Relations and crisis management;
- Executive interviews with the news media and financial markets.

These are still the driving applications for live corporate communications. They feature time sensitive information and typically include or require audience participation and interaction. This content is as valuable to a company as broadcast news, live sporting events, talk shows or other live events are to consumers. It is intended to provide impact and to obtain immediate results.

> **Home Depot** was credited for building a strong corporate culture during its early years, through a series of *Breakfast with Bernie and Arthur* town-hall meetings. The Breakfast meetings featured company founders Bernie Marcus and Arthur Blank. They were held every few months and originated live from different store locations; typically those celebrating a Grand Opening or other notable events. The programs were interactive, where employees asked questions of the hosts, and included pre-produced videos of store achievements or employee profiles.

Johnson & Johnson – Action and Response to 1982 Tylenol Scare

During the fall of 1982, seven people in the Chicago area died from taking cyanide-laced capsules which were put into Tylenol Extra-Strength packages and placed on retail shelves by a still unknown assailant(s). Johnson & Johnson, the parent company of McNeil Consumer Products, which makes Tylenol, was confronted with a crisis capable of seriously damaging the company.

Once the Tylenol containers were identified as the common thread for the seven deaths, Johnson & Johnson reacted quickly. The company established a two-phase strategy, putting customer safety first. The company immediately worked with law enforcement agencies and all news media channels to alert the public to not consume any Tylenol products and recalled every capsule. This action included several live press conferences and television interviews featuring Johnson & Johnson chairman, James Burke and other key executives, which originated from the company's corporate headquarters.

Within weeks Johnson & Johnson implemented the next phase of its strategy: to save the product. On November 11, 1982, the company conducted a live announcement from its headquarters to introduce its new safety seal, tamper resistant packaging. Media representatives were invited to hotel meeting rooms throughout the country to view the broadcast and learn about the promotional campaign to bring Tylenol back to market.

Johnson & Johnson's handling of the Tylenol tampering incident is widely considered one of the best examples of public relations crisis management in history. Although the company lost an estimated one-hundred million dollars by recalling some 31 million containers of Tylenol, the product was saved and the company brand protected.

"...What Johnson & Johnson executives have done is communicate the message that the company is candid, contrite, and compassionate, committed to solving the murders and protecting the public."

Washington Post

"The Tylenol crisis is without a doubt the most exemplary case ever known in the history of crisis communications. Any business executive, who has ever stumbled into a public relations ambush, ought to appreciate the way Johnson & Johnson responded to the Tylenol poisonings. They have effectively demonstrated how major business has to handle a disaster."[14]

The First 24-Hours (1990)

---

14 Berge, T. (1990). *The First 24-Hour*. Cambridge, MA: Basil Blackwell, Inc.

Content is King

Merrill Lynch – Responds to Wall Street's Black Monday

On October 19, 1987, the Dow Jones Industrial Average plunged 508.33 points to 1,738.74 earning the title: *Black Monday*. Many financial institutions and investment firms used their enterprise video networks during the following days to communicate with employees as well as customers. Although the video broadcasts cannot be credited with turning the market around, they are considered a critical component to providing confidence and guidance to clients who lost a significant percentage of their investments and brokers who would earn less in commissions.

On October 17, 1988, a year following Black Monday, Merrill Lynch & Co. outlined a two-pronged strategy for living in the post-crash world in a special global broadcast titled "One Year Later: Investing in a New Era."

The program originated from the company's New York headquarters and included live feeds from Merrill Lynch offices in London and Tokyo. It was viewed by employees and clients at 478 company offices and 70 additional meeting sites throughout North America.

During the broadcast, senior executives first addressed investor concerns, expressing optimism that financial markets were positioned for a rebound.

In ads leading up to the event, Merrill Lynch claimed "*On October 17th investors all across America will stop looking backward and start looking forward.*" Merrill Lynch credited the broadcast with providing clients with confidence in the company to manage their investments.

Edward Jones - Message to Field & Clients Following 9/11 Attacks

It is inevitable that most organizations have occasions where they are required to deal with unscheduled,

Digital Touch Points

difficult situations. The September 11, 2001 (9/11) terrorist attack was one of those times.

The managing partner of Edward Jones, John Bachmann, happened to be in New York on 9/11. He saw the need to immediately address the situation with the company's associates and customers.

Within hours of the attacks, Bachmann was in a rental car, driving to Columbus, SC, where the next day, he spoke to the Edward Jones associates from the studio of South Carolina Educational Television (SCET). Immediately following the broadcast, Bachman travelled to Dallas for a business commitment the next day. However, prior to the meeting he went to a local broadcast facility, where he spoke to and interacted with Edward Jones customers. In both programs, Bachmann described the scene in New York and discussed what it meant to Edward Jones and its customers.

Both broadcasts were backhauled to the company's headquarters in St. Louis and distributed over the Edward Jones video network. The quick, proactive action provided comfort and stability to the company's associates and customers.

Rollins Inc. provides pest and termite control services to residential and commercial customers in the United States and global markets. Rollins University is the company's learning organization, responsible for providing training to its 10,000 employees. Rollins University uses a wide range of methods, including instructor-led classroom training, technology-based training (CBT, virtual classroom), self-directed training, on-the-job training, and its interactive distance learning network: RollinsTV.[15]

RollinsTV leverages the company's proprietary network to provide about 40 hours of live training each week to

---

[15] *Rollins Corporation Takes Learning Global,* (December 2012) Globecommsystems.com

Content is King

500 of its field offices. All training is interactive, including the on-demand courses. In addition, RollinsTV uses the public Internet to extend the reach of its training to other offices including global affiliates.

The initial implementation of the RollinsTV network was financially justified based solely on cost avoidance, primarily by the offset of travel, lodging and employee (travel time) costs.

Collaborative and social media tools, the expanded use of videoconference and telepresence systems, desktop video and mobile devices have improved and extended the reach of live video-based communications, increasing digital touch points.

Is it Live or On-Demand

In the early 1970s, tape producer Memorex entered the consumer market with a campaign titled, "Is it live, or is it Memorex?" The company's television commercials featured Ella Fitzgerald who sang a note that shattered a glass while being recorded to a Memorex audio cassette. The tape was played back and the recording also broke the glass, prompting the question: "Is it live, or is it Memorex?"

Today, a more appropriate question may be is it live or on-demand?

> "Is it live, or is it Me~~m~~rex on-demand?"

This is an excellent example of the different taxonomy between groups or business units. The training and learning organizations may ask "is it synchronous or asynchronous?"[16]

A good amount of corporate content is not time sensitive. Some messages may enjoy a companywide notification and implementation window of months. Other information and

---

[16] Dr. Jolly Holden, and Dr. Philip Westfall, *An Instructional Media Selection Guide for Distance Learning - Implications for Blended Learning* (2010) FGDLA.org

training may have an extended or ongoing shelf-life of years. Fortunately, today's technology allows for a multitude of ways for employees to view content at their convenience: on-demand and on a variety of viewing devices. The quality of video-on-demand content can be comparable to or better than, live communications and can include some interactive functionality and full testing and analytics capabilities.

Examples of internal communications which are ideal for delayed or on-demand applications are:

- Employee on-boarding;
- Training modules and sessions;
- "How to" videos;
- Product information;
- Employee profiles;
- Company success stories;
- Town-hall meetings and executive messages.

In addition, making content available for on-demand access allows employees the opportunity to view content multiple times, functioning as a refresher or reminder.

As covered in Chapter 6: *Blend Enterprise-wide Digital Media Channels*, a company needs to implement the right type and blend of media technology to meet its entire communication and training objectives.

Right Amount of Relevant Content

It is equally important to provide the right amount of relevant content. What does this mean? First, and foremost, know your target audience(s). Are they:

- Internal - Company employees:
  Office staff, sales associates, executives, field representatives, union employees, management, branch or store managers?

Content is King

- External – Customers, prospective customers, news media, financial markets or other external audiences?

Second, thoroughly understand the objective(s) of the program or meeting and the time and effort to effectively and successfully convey the message. For internal communications:

- All-employee town-hall meetings may be lengthy, but due to their nature, are typically infrequent.
- Executive messages and updates should be brief and as frequent as the subject dictates.
- Training sessions are dictated by many factors, including:
  - Subject;
  - Type and number of participants;
  - Locations of participants (e.g.: time zones);
  - Fit and role of content in over-all lesson plan (e.g.: what are other training tools, pre-requisite or supplementary classes);
  - Initial or continuing education classes may require multiple, long days;
  - Follow-up and supplementary training may be executed effectively with brief updates or modules.

Schedule communications with respect to employee schedules, workload and need to know, taking into account other communications and activities directed at the same individuals. Do not overwhelm employees with content. Too much too often may negatively impact their ability to perform their jobs.

> Too much employee-directed content, provided too often, can be ineffective!

Service Company – A leading service company implemented a video network to hundreds of its key locations. The company provided timely and relevant corporate and marketing communications as well as training for management and staff. Initial results were very positive as the managers embraced the opportunity to receive information and timely updates from corporate. Unfortunately, the amount of content increased, to the where it was nearly overwhelming the staff and impacting their ability to perform their jobs. Fortunately, branch managers worked with corporate to identify the right balance of content and amount of time to allocate for communications and training.

Just because the company has communication channels do not feel obligated to broadcast 24x7 like the major television or cable networks.

Customers / Consumers Want Content

Customers and other external audiences will only consume content when and how it is of interest. Based on the assumption that most externally directed on-line content is viewed on-demand, it is unlikely that too much information can be provided about a company, its products or services.

For best results, video content should feature a single item or topic and be brief, typically 30 to 90 seconds. The number of video clips can be unlimited, based on the extent of the information the company has to convey. Each clip should be properly titled and supported by relevant descriptive information.

The video content should be easily accessible, and be supported with accurate naming conventions. The content should be strategically placed on company and/or third-party websites. Videos should be complemented with links to other video clips or associated documentation.

Bottom-line, provide clear, concise and compelling content that encourages action that:

- ➢ Results in on-line purchases;
- ➢ Directs viewers to other on-line products and services for up-selling;
- ➢ Increases visits to retail outlets for on-premise purchases.

The in-store experience should be similar to the on-line viewing of video content. Digital signage and interactive displays will provide video clips on products and services, supplemented by associated information. The objective is to motivate customers to compare the in-store content to what they have researched on their personal devices and drive them to the checkout counter. Video clips intended to inform and to demonstrate products may be 30 to 90 seconds. The duration of clips to inspire point-of-purchase sales should be very short, typically in the three to five second range.

All actions can be tracked by content and the individual's viewing habits and purchases. Based on analytics, a company can identify and create video content to the format and approaches proven to achieve the best results.

> Customer and other external-directed content should be brief, but the number can be limitless!

The news media and financial markets are a different story. Primarily, they are interested in live interviews with executives and subject matter experts. Also, they welcome recorded footage (B-roll) of natural disasters or news-worthy incidents impacting communities and a company's business. On occasion, they may broadcast company provided common interest stories, especially on a local level. Although live interviews may run longer, all produced content should be short, typically from 15 seconds to 90 seconds. This approach is the same that has been embraced by the broadcast community for decades in local and national newscasts.

If the Content is Applicable, Use It Time and Time Again

Product shots, executive interviews, employee profiles and success stories, historical footage of special events, facilities, products and television commercials are good examples of video content which can be used for a variety of applications

Digital Touch Points

across different media channels and directed at a wide range of target audiences.

In today's environment, where employees throughout the company are recording video content, everyone should be encouraged to use existing media.

Also, it is very common for companies to re-purpose recorded footage of live meetings, training sessions and executive interviews into short, modular segments for on-demand viewing.

Digital asset management and archiving systems feature naming and tagging functionality, which enable the easy search and access of content. The content is edited to tell the additional story(s), possibly many times and ways for different audiences, then transcoded (formatted) for distribution to numerous type display devices.

By having the right systems to preserve and protect video assets and the staffing resources to name and manage the content, a company can enjoy significant costs savings by re-purposing it for multiple uses. This will allow the company to avoid unnecessary production costs and travel expenses to shoot the same or similar footage. Also, the re-purposing of available content can decrease the time to get information to market, possibly realizing revenue opportunities sooner.

> Leverage Good Content Across All Viable Audiences.

Whence it Comes? The Conundrum!

To meet the demand for video, companies are producing more content than ever. And, as with people electing to view content when and where they want, companies are originating content from virtually anywhere. This is good and bad.

There are more sources and means to feed the beast cost effectively, including the utilization of every camera or device with access into the corporate infrastructure: two-way

Content is King

videoconference and telepresence systems, desktops, executive and insert flashcam studios, laptops and mobile devices.

These systems can be located anywhere: to originate content from corporate headquarters or regional and field offices, manufacturing plants or retail outlets, home offices, client facilities, domestic or global.

Also, most everyone in the company is a potential contributor as some employees will shoot, edit and distribute company related content. This is commonly referred to as "employee-generated content (EGC)."

Employees can record business related or newsworthy events as they happen. This can be an inexpensive way for companies to ensure that activities are documented for brand, legal or motivational applications. Also, this can save companies time and money by avoiding the need to send production crews to the field and incur travel costs. Now the conundrum.

People and departments are seduced by the sexiness and allure of video communications. As stated earlier, any employee may feel empowered to produce content about the company. They may use consumer level systems, which generally provide good video quality but less than acceptable audio. However, the quality of production values tend to be far less professional than content produced by the company's video organization. The videos may be uploaded to the company's websites, YouTube and other online video websites without prior corporate approval and often are outside of the company's brand policies. This user-generated content is considered by some to be "renegade video."

In some ways, we are experiencing a bit of the "Wild West" as anyone can shoot video and distribute content via the pubic Internet. The primary issue may be who is watching the store, protecting the corporate brand?

Although the quality of employee-produced video may not meet the standards of company productions, the value of the content will dictate its use. In some cases, it may find a large audience.

This is due to public video web sites, as well as the news networks, which allow a wider range of quality acceptance by viewers.

It is critical that companies publish branding standards and the video or communication organization establishes production guidelines. All uses of the content should be governed to ensure the company is not exposed to litigation, instances of negative public relations or the compromising of its brand.

Tips and Perspectives

- Content is King!
  Let it drive the selection of media and technology solutions.

- Content must be relevant and compelling!
  Do not waste the time of employees or lose sales by leaving customers unsatisfied.

- Do not be wowed by technology:
  Select the technology which best supports and enhances the presentation of the message(s) and as determined by results of a well-thought-out enterprise-wide media business strategy.

  Implementing the wrong technology for any reason can be costly.

- Use video to demonstrate company and industry-wide best practices:
  It can significantly reduce the amount of initial training required.

- Live or on-demand?
  Go with live when it needs to be timely, interactive or motivational.

  Use on-demand for most anything else, including the re-feed or re-purposing of live content.

- Re-edit and re-use relevant content:

Make it available to, and easy to access by, all authorized users.

Enjoy cost savings by avoiding multiple recordings of same or similar content.

Realize revenue gains by getting content to market sooner.

- Do not overwhelm employees with too much content:
  Be respectful of their time and resources.
- Provide customer and public directed content often:
  Keep it fresh.
- Focus on providing short segments and modules.
- Encourage the creation and origination of content from all employee sources.
- Establish brand and video production guidelines and policies:
  Protect the company brand and manage the video production workflow.

Digital Touch Points

Chapter 4

Establish a Media Business Strategy

Incorporate Media Strategies into Business Plan

Video and dynamic media can be educational, informative and sometimes entertaining. Ideally, they are also inspirational and motivational, improving employee performance and driving sales. Now that video and dynamic media have achieved mainstream recognition as important means to communicate, train and market, companies should ensure their proper utilization by developing a media business strategy.

The media business strategy should take into account the media and communication needs of all groups including the marketing, training and learning organizations and communications and media departments. It should be thoroughly integrated into the company's over-all business strategy. It should be inclusive of the criteria addressed in any business strategy, but that which is specifically relevant to the use of media for marketing, training and communication applications.

The media business strategy should clearly identify:

- All target audiences the company needs to reach, inclusive of:
  - Employees;
  - Customers and prospective customers;

  Commercial advertising campaigns and activities should be factored into the strategy.
- What is the message(s)?
  What do you want them to know?
- When do you need to reach them?
  What is the timeframe to achieve the goal?
- What do you want them to feel?
- What do you want them to do?

Digital Touch Points

These are criteria that should be familiar to marketing organizations and, to some degree, to training and learning groups. The strategy needs to take into account that many goals will be different for the internal targeted audiences than the external.

It is critical that everyone is on the same page. They should recognize that the use of video and dynamic media works across multiple functional groups and can drive revenue and impact the company's bottom line.

The strategy should span three to five years, based on the company's specific business practice as applied to the goals of each group. Also, the strategy should provide a realistic expectation of how long it will take to plan, implement and measure the results.

The media business strategy should be supported by a business plan and media implementation strategy. They should be inclusive of the communication requirements of all departments and business units and be leveraged across all media channels throughout the company. They should identify the best approach(es) to select and implement the right blend of technology, resources and workflow to support the company's business objectives.

Implement the Media Channels

The business plan and media implementation strategy are more than simply the implementation of a channel or two. They should address:

- ➢ Content design and creation and/or acquisition and ingest of third-party content;
- ➢ Interfacing with a wide range of distinct and possibly disparate systems, which may be operated by different departments and business units;
- ➢ The convergence, blending and unification of content from all systems, to all sources, with the involvement in and management by multiple administrators;

Establish a Media Business Strategy

- That it is not just technology or a good cost model;
- It is where solutions and systems for internal communications and training are also used for external communications for consumer-facing applications on-line, in-store or on the move using smart phones and tablets.

Here are a number of key items to factor into the strategy:

- All departments and functional groups touch or are touched by video;
- Video is digital, therefore, data. To IT, it is just another application;
- Consider all components in the entire video ecosystem to ensure they function to maximum proficiency once implemented;
- Get guidance and support from video-centric vendors who understand video applications, systems and issues;
- Implement guidelines and policies to govern the workflow and protect the brand;
- Leverage the ability to collect and use viewer analytics;
- Carefully develop the business model. Factor in the justification to communicate versus the cost of NOT embracing video communications!

As TV and Computers Have Converged
So has Video and IT...and Marketing, Sales, Real Estate, Facilities, etc.

The convergence of television and computers (video and data), has had a significant impact on companies and everyone involved with video communications. For those who use and produce video content, the convergence provides a welcome change. For some of those in IT (information technology) and telecom organizations, it may not be as welcome as it should be. Once video advanced from analog to digital formats, and the consumer space embraced the use of computers and personal devices to view and share video content, the video freight train had left the station.

Simply put, video is another application which runs over IT managed networks. People in all roles and departments are using video, including: executives, marketing, sales, public relations and training groups. Other departments such as real estate, facilities and operations are factoring video systems and display screens into building construction and office re-locations. Items such as large digital display screens are now factored into their budgets as furniture and facility expenses. Procurement and legal departments are purchasing video and media solutions as managed services. This approach is similar to how companies have traditionally purchased data and communication solutions. Managed services are covered in Chapter 9: *Managed Video as a Service.*

Get Everyone on the Same Page

As a result of convergence, the emergence of social media and the blurring of lines between the internal and external communities, it is critical that media, IT and other key departments align their efforts. For a media business strategy to be successful there is the need to:

- Have all stakeholders and functional support groups on the same page regarding the value of media;
- Know and embrace the role of video and dynamic media in the company;
- Understand the impact and value it can have toward meeting business outcomes;
- Implement fully integrated solutions across the organization.

> It's not just technology or having a good cost model.
> It's knowing how the tools and solutions will be used and that everyone is on board!

Establish a Media Business Strategy

As depicted in the diagram below, visual communications plays a compelling role in the realm of voice, data and video communications.

Blending of Communication Channels Across User and Functional Groups

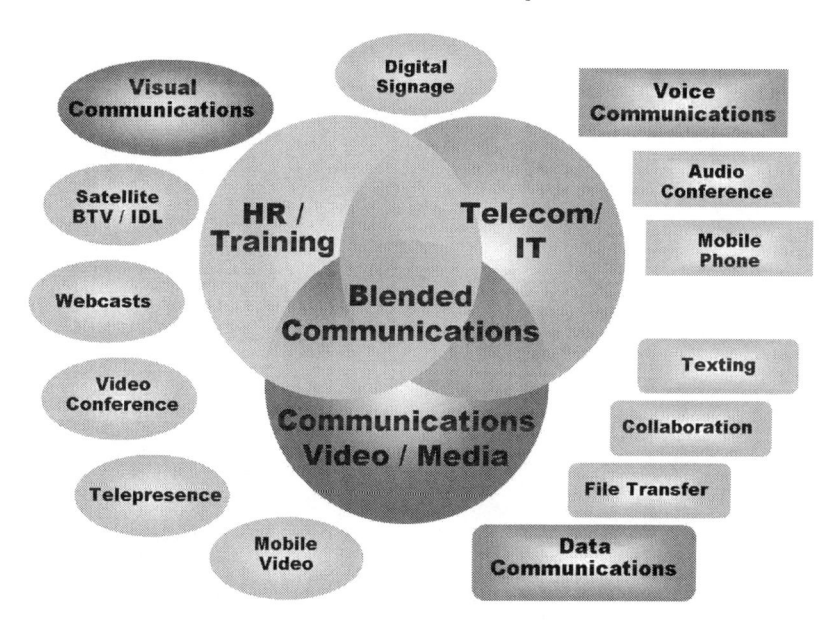

[Diagram: Blended Communications showing overlapping circles of HR/Training, Telecom/IT, and Communications Video/Media, surrounded by: Visual Communications, Digital Signage, Voice Communications, Satellite BTV/IDL, Audio Conference, Mobile Phone, Webcasts, Texting, Video Conference, Collaboration, Telepresence, File Transfer, Mobile Video, Data Communications]

The cohesive outcome should be a sustainable strategy that is cost effective and successful in touching all targeted audiences: internal and external. At a minimum, it should include:

➢ Thorough analysis of existing production capabilities and media channels;
➢ Driving applications for:
  o Communications;
  o Training and learning;
  o Digital signage;
  o Marketing and merchandising (online & in-store);
➢ A content strategy for:
  o Internal and external audiences;
  o Live and video-on-demand applications.

Consider the communication types as addressed in Chapter 3: *Content is King.*

- ➤ Facilities and systems, including both existing and projected upgrades and build-outs:
  - Production studios and field systems to high definition (HDTV) and ultra high definition (UHD);
  - Delivery systems and approaches;
  - Display systems and solutions for:
    - Digital signage;
    - Group viewing environments;
    - Individual and/or small group viewing;
    - Mobile devices;
  - Auditoriums, conference rooms and training centers;
  - Audiovisual and media systems;
  - Videoconference and telepresence systems.
- ➤ Delivery Options:
  - Satellite;
  - Terrestrial;
  - Wireless.

  Including wide area and local area networks for broadcast, multicast, webcast, streaming, video-on-demand, etc.
- ➤ Staffing resources to:
  - Produce, manage, track and govern the workflow and content;
  - Operate systems;
  - Provide consultative customer support services;
  - Research, design and integrate system build-outs and upgrades;
  - Manage and maintain systems;
  - Manage outsourced vendors.

Communication, Training and Marketing Requirements

How to Contribute to the Business Objectives and Improve the Bottom Line

As the value of video-based communications, training and marketing has increased, it has become as mission critical to some companies as data applications. Video and dynamic media has earned a "place at the table." This is achieved by developing a compelling media business strategy and business model.

The departments responsible for internal communications and training and the departments responsible for marketing and merchandising to external audiences should collaborate to find a single, unified media solution. Of course, this can include multiple systems from a variety of vendors. It is counter productive to work in silos and not cost effective to maintain repetitive systems.

In many companies, the video, media and communication departments perform as functional support groups to assist training and marketing efforts. This should enhance the opportunities for collaboration and success.

The relevant business objectives as well as functional, operational and technical requirements should be well-articulated and substantiated in the business and implementation plan. This will enhance the probability of receiving executive approval and gain support from the IT organization.

Video is Just Another Application:
Get Comfortable with It

Gone are the days where video was a bandwidth hog and IT organizations were justified in keeping it off the company network. Today, video is a data application, and by utilizing advanced video compression and other technology, it can efficiently and securely traverse IT and telecommunication networks. In addition, terrestrial infrastructure continues to expand, broadening the bandwidth pipe and reaching further into the "have not" areas and global markets cost effectively.

It is important that members of the IT organization be as comfortable with video and dynamic media uses and systems as they are with data applications. This is achievable due to the probability that many of them are personally well-versed in video. They are likely to create and view on-line video and play interactive video games at home and on their personal devices. These individuals could apply this perspective to the workplace and support video applications over the enterprise networks.

Best-of-breed companies are engaging video and media-centric industry vendors to obtain guidance and solutions. These vendors have experience with, and better understanding of, how to securely interoperate video-based systems into IT and network infrastructure.

Video Ecosystem is Robust and Flourishing
Leverage it Widely and Wisely to Get Results!

Today's video and dynamic media solutions consist of numerous distinct, yet interoperable, components. When integrated and operated correctly, they constitute a robust and powerful communications system from content creation and development, to publishing and delivery, content and network administrative capabilities to content management and archiving, testing and polling to tracking results and analytics.

The digital asset management and archiving solution should be treated as the core of enterprise communications. It will have a significant impact on media workflow throughout the organization including archiving, metadata and retrieval of relevant content.

Successful companies are implementing complementary systems over the three-to-five year plan. They are phasing them in as funding dictates and following a life-cycle plan for upgrades and replacement. Many of the early adopters are executing this approach under the auspices of managed services where the vendor is responsible for the system, service and future-proofing.

Look to Media-centric Providers
For Video and Dynamic Media Solutions

Vendors of video-based solutions have provided capable and effective equipment and services for decades. This includes production and editing systems, compression, encoding and transcoding systems, analog and digital transmission systems, satellite and terrestrial networks for broadcast and IP multicast applications and interactive distance learning systems. There is a wide selection of robust and affordable solutions available.

Based on a company's specific requirements and usage, different equipment and software solutions will provide more value. Fortunately, the industry is served by a large number of viable providers offering solutions with a wide variety of features, functionality and overall capabilities. Companies should have confidence that one or more of these vendors and their respective solution sets can meet their video ecosystem requirements. It is likely that they are inclusive of bundled, fully-integrated systems from multiple sources which may provide best-of-breed solutions. However, this approach is not ideal for every company and the benefits should be weighed against unbundled, home-grown solutions and self-managed services.

Companies can benefit from video vendors' knowledge and expertise by leveraging their experiences and lessons learned from the implementation of other, multiple enterprise-wide systems.

To use a century's old idiom, get it "straight from the horse's mouth."

Governance – Protect the Brand and Video Workflow

It is critical that companies establish branding standards and production guidelines for the recording and placement of video content, especially as it relates to external-facing applications. A few key areas are to:

- Develop video production (quality standards) guidelines and approval channels;
- Establish guidelines which outline when and how employees should engage the corporate video group for assistance;
- Clearly define and establish a video production workflow process (from content creation through delivery and analysis);
- Address legal issues and considerations related to:
  - Digital rights management;
  - Use of images and likenesses – subject/talent approvals;
  - Brand references and representations.

Governance and the enforcement of the guidelines and policies will ensure the company is not exposed to avoidable incidents or legal issues.

The Business Model

Justify and Recognize Improved ROI!

The use of video is up for consumers and the enterprise space. The cost of equipment, software, support services and incremental usage are down. It is a combination that corporate and financial executive's desire: More for less!

As a result, justifying the cost of today's video-based solutions and services is less of a challenge. The focus is on how to select and implement the right blend of systems and associated workflow into the existing infrastructure.

Once executives identify their marketing, communications and training needs, they should work with the IT organization to locate viable solutions and establish budgetary funding requirements. The IT group can provide insight and financial models to craft the media business strategy and establish cost justifications.

Establish a Media Business Strategy

By leveraging media channels and resources across all stakeholders, successful companies are finding that the costs to create, manage, deliver and display content are affordable. The calculated return on investment (ROI) may be so favorable that a company finds the cost of effective communications is less than what they spend on employee coffee.

Tips and Perspectives

- Invest the time and resources to develop a media business strategy.
- Identify all video applications, users and media channels.
- Identify the company's communication, marketing and training requirements:
- Get buy-in and support from executives, users and functional groups.
- Get everyone in the organization on the same page:
  Taxonomy varies between groups. Make sure everyone has a clear understanding of what others are thinking and saying.
- Build the business model:
  Based on a thorough understanding of the company's video needs and other factors addressed in the media business strategy, it should provide a compelling justification for investment.

  The cost to communicate via video per employee may be less than the cost to provide coffee.
- Understand and consider the entire video ecosystem:
  It is a series of computers interfaced with the network and media channels.

  Establish a strategy to manage equipment, implementation and resource costs.
- Future-proof your investment:

For long-term sustainability, with considerations for video applications and requirements, company culture, infrastructure, industry and technology trends.

- Benchmark against best-of-breed, bleeding edge enterprise organizations.
- Engage the services of an industry specialist to:
  Assist with the media business strategy;
  Provide industry knowledge and perspective;
  Provide structure, processes and guidance;
  Conduct a gap analysis of systems, capabilities and resources;
  Save time, internal resources and money.
- Video is digital, therefore, data:
  It should be embraced by IT as just another application.
- Vendor role and value:
  Get guidance and support from video-centric vendors;

  Leverage relationships with existing vendors (those who are your trusted advisors);

  Caution against vendors claiming they have the ability to do everything. There are situations where it is best to acquire:
  Bundled solutions and services;
  Unbundled, home-grown solutions.
- Governance:
  Implement guidelines and policies to govern workflow and protect the brand;

  Establish guidelines and processes to track and measure the use and success of your media channels.
- Analytics:
  Leverage the ability to collect and use viewer and participant analytics.
- Select the right solution(s) to meet your business as well as functional, operational and technical requirements:

Do not let technology drive application decisions!

Chapter 5

Viewing Locations and Environments

Where are your targeted viewers?
Where are they most likely to view your content?

The answers to these two basic questions may seem parochial to some. However, they can have a significant impact on how effective companies are in providing effective, successful communications and achieving improved business results.

Properly addressing viewing locations and devices are critical components to empowering your viewers: encouraging them to consume your content and/or motivating them to purchase your company's products and services.

Viewing Locations: Reach Them Where it Counts!

Think holistically! Take into consideration employees throughout the entire organization, as well as all prospective customers (online and in-store). This should include wholesale and retail markets, strategic partners, key suppliers and the news media. In today's global society, internal and external targeted viewers are as likely to be 10 to 12 time zones away as they are to be in the same state or region. It may be a diverse and widely dispersed group, but do not be overwhelmed. There are media tools and delivery solutions which can allow you to reach them all, in a timely and consistent manner. And importantly, the solutions are affordable!

The first point of consideration is geographic distribution: domestic and international. Both will have areas with an abundance of bandwidth, where access is relatively easy to achieve. Other areas, including those in the U.S. may present challenges. However, satellite and wireless technologies can ensure the reach of proprietary or Internet access virtually anywhere.

Digital Touch Points

On-Premise Group, Public or Individual Settings

Next, it is important to understand the type of facility and the room or area where the content will be viewed. It is equally important to know if the content will be viewed in group settings or individually. Why are these critical issues?

> **Not all content is equal.**
> It may require different delivery considerations, display environments and interactive capabilities.

While content may be king, all content is not created equal! Company-wide live town-hall meetings are typically viewed on display screens by most employees in auditoriums and large public areas such as lobbies, cafeterias and meeting rooms. Some viewing takes place at individual work stations, especially in small offices or off-site facilities. An increasing number of employees are viewing live meetings on personal devices. Departmental and functional group meetings are also likely to include both group and individual participation.

Group settings and interactive communications will foster a higher degree of audience participation, which can contribute to building a collaborative corporate culture and enhance the viewer experience.

Group viewing is also beneficial for live training and information sessions which do not require hands-on participation. Especially, when enhanced through interactive communications and the ability to conduct tests and surveys during and following the sessions.

Due to telecommuting and the increased mobility of today's workforce, a growing number of workers view content at workstations or on mobile devices. Although some content may be viewed live, it is more likely to be viewed when convenient to these individuals. Interactivity is still possible in these scenarios, but on a delayed basis. Taking tests and responding to surveys are also possible.

Viewing Locations and Environments

The following graphic provides examples of viewing environments which may be applicable to different facilities and locations. Those listed in the center are common to most facilities. A few unique viewing environments are listed (in boxed text) with their respective facility type. Field sales and service representatives will utilize mobile devices and also utilize many of the listed facility viewing areas.

Environments for Targeted Viewers

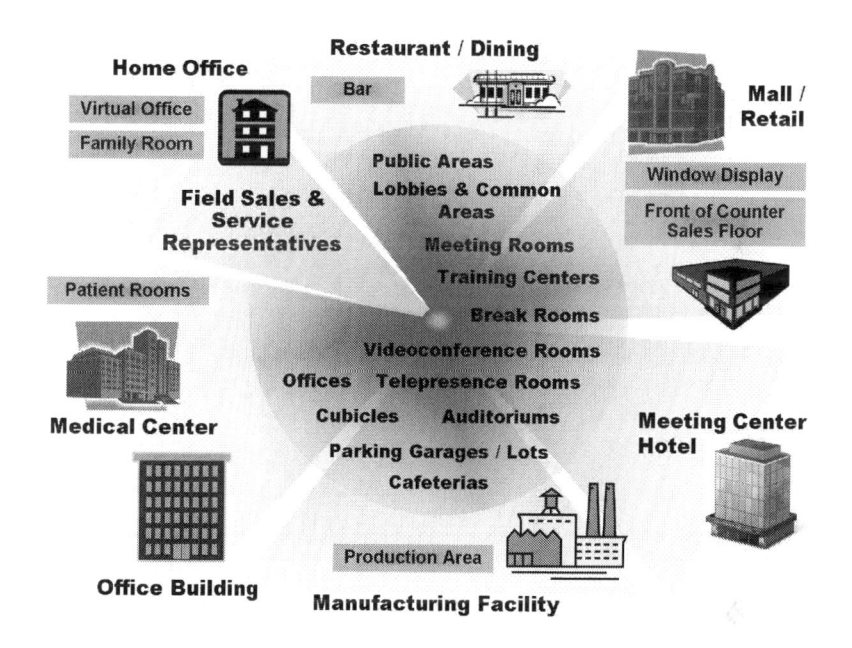

Home Office
- Virtual Office
- Family Room

Restaurant / Dining
- Bar

Mall / Retail
- Window Display
- Front of Counter Sales Floor

Field Sales & Service Representatives

Patient Rooms

Medical Center

Office Building

Public Areas
Lobbies & Common Areas
Meeting Rooms
Training Centers
Break Rooms
Videoconference Rooms
Offices Telepresence Rooms
Cubicles Auditoriums
Parking Garages / Lots
Cafeterias

Meeting Center Hotel

Production Area

Manufacturing Facility

Consumers/customers are like telecommuters or field personnel, in that they will view content at personal workstations or on their mobile devices. In addition to viewing a company's website(s), their on-line experience is enhanced through research and competitive on-line shopping and the use of social media to interact with and share content with friends.

It is critical to provide the right content in the format and quality best suited for the respective viewing devices to ensure an engaging experience. For example, news and information can be displayed on monitors and/or flat panel display screens

Digital Touch Points

throughout facilities, including lobbies, elevators, cafeterias and other common areas. In retail environments, advertising, marketing and other promotional content can be displayed on screens at point-of-sale/purchase (POS) locations. The objective is to use everything possible to drive customers to action: to purchase goods and services.

The various media channels provide companies the ability to track viewing and interactions and collect analytics. This allows companies the opportunity to further hone the message and improve business results.

Communicate to All Employees, Not Just Most

For decades, enterprise organizations were satisfied, if not elated, to reach a majority of their employees with corporate communications and training in real-time. For the purpose of this example, we will use 80 percent (80%) as the typical amount. Depending on their geographic footprint, companies achieved the 80% by using satellite-based business television networks and two-way videoconferencing systems. The remaining 20 percent (20%) were likely to be in remote areas and locations with few employees. Therefore, they were excluded from live communications due to the then high cost of network connectivity. These individuals received the same content via less timely or inconvenient means such as: videotape or DVD, print documents, audio conferencing, on-site meetings (road-shows) or travel to corporate or regional offices. The content delivery approach for companies without networks consisted of the same options. Also, during this period, the idea of reaching global audiences was limited to only a small percentage of companies.

> Follow the "80-20 Rule" although it now may be "95-5"

Now, expectations are much higher. A company should strive to reach all of its employees with live, real-time content. But for

Viewing Locations and Environments

the sake of reason, target a minimum of 95%. Why is this possible and how?

> Bandwidth is available and affordable to reach virtually anywhere, whether by terrestrial, satellite or wireless delivery;
> Display screens and devices are everywhere;
> Content can be delivered via open systems, e.g.: to any device via any operating system.

> If Consumers can view YouTube content and Internet videos on their own devices...
>
> **Employees** should be able to view company provided video communications and training content on company provided or approved devices!
>
> **Customers** should be able to view company branded information and merchandizing content!

More important, employees in distant and hard to reach locations are less likely to accept the excuse that it is too difficult to deliver live communications to them. How can it be, when they are able to access video and rich media content via their personal computers and mobile devices?

Tips and Perspectives

♦ Know your target audience(s) and where they are located. *Think holistically. Be all inclusive!*

♦ Strive to reach all employees, regardless of location: *The Internet is global and everyone may be a prospective customer.*

The effort alone will increase and improve company morale.

Everyone wants to be included.

Digital Touch Points

- Foster an environment of engagement and sharing:
  Leverage the benefits of group and individual viewing as well as the collaborative nature of social media.

- Provide viewing options:
  Enable the ability to view content where and on the screen of choice;

  Large screen displays in group settings, at desktops, on mobile devices.

- Informed and educated viewers will result in:
  Improved employee performance;
  Increased market visibility;
  Improved brand image;
  Increased sales.

Chapter 6

Blend Digital Media Channels

Leverage Channels and Resources to Maximize ROI

New and evolving technologies are dramatically impacting the way we access and view information, as consumers as well as in the workplace. The Internet and enterprise-wide intranets and extranets are complementing established terrestrial and satellite-based distribution networks.

Large digital display screens are everywhere: the home, malls and retail stores, branch offices, meeting and hospitality facilities, airports, entertainment parks, etc.

Wireless networks and mobile devices are delivering content to consumers and employees anytime, anywhere. Depending on the individual, and his or her situation, video content is consumed on a selection of screens, of varying sizes, live or at the viewer's convenience.

We have talked about the convergence of technologies (video and data) and the blurring of media channels to reach internal and external audiences. Now, we are going to address how and why companies are blending their digital media channels and resources to increase digital touch points.

Companies are advertising, marketing and promoting their products and services to consumers via digital media: on-line from home, in-store and virtually anywhere in-between and on different display screens. Similar, if not the same, digital media are used to educate, inform and train employees using internal and on-premise channels. The technologies for both consumer and corporate applications are essentially built on the same platforms and form factors. This includes televisions, computers and mobile devices. It also includes the systems used to encode, transmit and receive content. As an example, the cable TV set-top box or satellite receiver in the home is very similar to the device(s) used in the corporate environment.

Therefore, it is only logical that companies should aggregate their technologies and infrastructure to work across all internal and external channels, including the Cloud.

Best-of-breed companies are using their business and implementation plans to perform as the guideline for corporate technology initiatives related to media channels and resources. This includes:

- Collaboration across user and functional support groups;
- Implementation of an enterprise-wide solution;
- Utilization of a hybrid delivery solution (when appropriate);
- Allocation of funding responsibility to appropriate parties;
- Allocation and training of staff resources.

Cross-Functional Collaboration
Blended Media and Unified Effort

A successful implementation of blended media is more than the convergence of media channels, displays and associated systems. It is getting stakeholders throughout the company to work together rather than in silos. Collectively, everyone needs to be creative and think out-of-the-box about how to make the new media work for the entire organization.

Executives, marketing, sales and learning leaders need to push the envelope with their communication, media and IT staffs about new and different ways to provide real-time (live) and non-real-time communications. They should benchmark with peers in other organizations and confer with their communication and media groups to identify best-of-breed approaches, techniques and newly implemented solutions which can benefit their specific and unique challenges.

> **Content Providers:**
> Focus on the message, but bring fresh ideas and "Best Practices" to the discussion.

The communication and media organizations need to do the same. It is their responsibility to stay current with the video-based solutions to create, distribute, manage and display the content. More important, it is their role to provide consultative guidance and support to executives and other content providers such as the marketing department and training and learning organizations. They are the producers of the content and should have the best understanding of how to tell and present the stories: when, where and how to use hard media, audiovisual systems, live streaming, interactive tools, videoconferencing, etc. They should have a handle on the industry leading vendors and video solutions and work closely with the IT and telecomm organizations to identify media technology and software to operate over the company's network.

> **Media and Communication Professionals:**
> Support the executives and content providers as well as provide guidance and collaboration to the IT organization.

The training and learning organizations need to collaborate with their company's functional support groups to implement and utilize media channels to help them meet their learning objectives. They are responsible to design and develop content for their target audiences and should know best about the environment and instructional media best suited for learning. However, they may need assistance with the selection and implementation of the right blend of media channels. Dr. Jolly Holden and Dr. Philip Westfall provide an excellent description of blended learning and guidance for

Digital Touch Points

instructional media selection for distance learning in their publication *An Instructional Media Selection Guide for Distance Learning - Implications for Blended Learning.*[17]

> *"Each distance learning medium...has its strengths and weaknesses when supporting various instructional strategies. No single medium can support all instructional strategies."*
>
> Dr. Holden and Dr. Westfall

> No single medium can support all instructional strategies.

In this media-centric world, it is crucial that executives work closely with the IT and telecom organizations. IT and telecom groups need to accept the fact that video and dynamic media applications are here to stay. It is inevitable that the use of video will increase and expand throughout the company. Now that video is digital, and systems are computer based, it is IT's responsibility to ensure that the systems integrate with the infrastructure, without impeding or impacting the operation of other applications on the network. They should recognize that today's systems are more robust and easier to implement than legacy solutions and that they are affordable. Also, they should engage the communications and media groups for guidance and support related to all things video.

> **IT, Telecom** and other **Operational Groups:**
> Embrace the widespread use of video and focus on how best to implement and manage the solutions throughout the organization.

---

[17] Dr. Jolly Holden, and Dr. Philip Westfall, *An Instructional Media Selection Guide for Distance Learning - Implications for Blended Learning* (2010) USDLA.org

The collaboration and sharing of information across all user and functional groups will enhance the probability that the company will implement the right blend of systems and capabilities.

> **A company** asked for my assistance during the early period of smart phones to help justify the purchase of iPhones for each of its 1,000 branch managers. The business model we developed presented a compelling case to deliver video content in a cost-effective, timely manner. Unfortunately, four other departments in the company submitted requests in the same budget cycle for phones for the same branch managers. IT and facility groups requested BlackBerrys, primarily for voice and data applications. The marketing and training groups requested iPhones for video and rich media related applications.
>
> The result: All requests were turned down. The groups were instructed to get on the same page and identify a single phone to best meet the collective needs. The message: Get on the same page and avoid unnecessary expenses.

The Video Ecosystem: A Robust, Flexible Business Tool
Blend the Independent Components to Efficiently Manage Workflow

Today's video and dynamic media systems are robust, flexible, easy to implement and manage and are more affordable than imagined only a few years ago. They can include a wide range of equipment and systems, such as:

Capture and Produce: Cameras, recording devices and formats, edit systems, video switchers, audio consoles, and computer graphics systems are a few of the systems used to capture and produce content.

Distribution and Network Management: Media platforms, video servers, encoders, transcoders, video compression systems, network management systems

Digital Touch Points

and digital signage solutions are a few of the key components to distribute content and manage network performance.

Receive and Display: Video appliances (known as receivers, edge devices, set-top boxes, etc.), digital display screens, desktop computers and mobile devices receive, store, route and display the content.

Manage and Measure: Digital asset management and archiving systems, media platforms and interactive distance learning systems manage the content and track the network and user activity and learning results.

The following graphic provides examples of key elements by categories in the video ecosystem.

Video Ecosystem – Key Elements

Content Creation	Content Production Origination	Distribution	Receive & Display	Manage & Measure
Scheduling, Pre-Production, Field Production Edit, Copy and/or Modify to Create New Assets	Edit, Studio Production Graphics & Other Support Materials Video-conference Telepresence Desktop Video Mobile Devices Video Servers	Media Platforms Video Servers Encoders Transcoders Video Compression Digital Signage Systems Network Management	Video Appliances (Edge Devices, Set-top Boxes, etc.) Digital Display Screens Desktop Computers Tablets & Mobile Devices Wearable Devices	Digital Asset Management & Archiving Systems Media Platforms Interactive Distance Learning Systems

The list is extensive, especially when considering the different type of equipment, systems and software for each item. For instance, there are different cameras, based on the application: production studio; professional or industrial field systems and consumer cameras; security, loss prevention and gaze cameras, two-way videoconference and telepresence systems, desktop video, iPad and tablet cameras and smart phone cameras.

The same is true of display screens, where large LCD, LED, plasma and OLED screens are used in meeting and conference

Blend Digital Media Channels

rooms and classrooms for group viewing. Also, they are located in lobbies, cafeterias and public areas for digital signage applications. Desktop monitors are used for individual viewing as are laptops, tablets, phones and other mobile devices which may soon include smartwatches and Google Glass.

It is important to note that most everything is computer-based, allowing the devices to interface: work together. In essence, content can originate from virtually any of the systems, traverse internal and/or external networks using the same, if not similar, solutions and be displayed on virtually any viewing device.

Also, content designed for live, real-time communications can be delivered to a specific target audience and edited (re-purposed) for different uses and viewing by varying audiences at a later time (non-real-time or on-demand).

The following graphic provides a perspective of the Video Ecosystem.

Video Ecosystem
Digital Media Channels

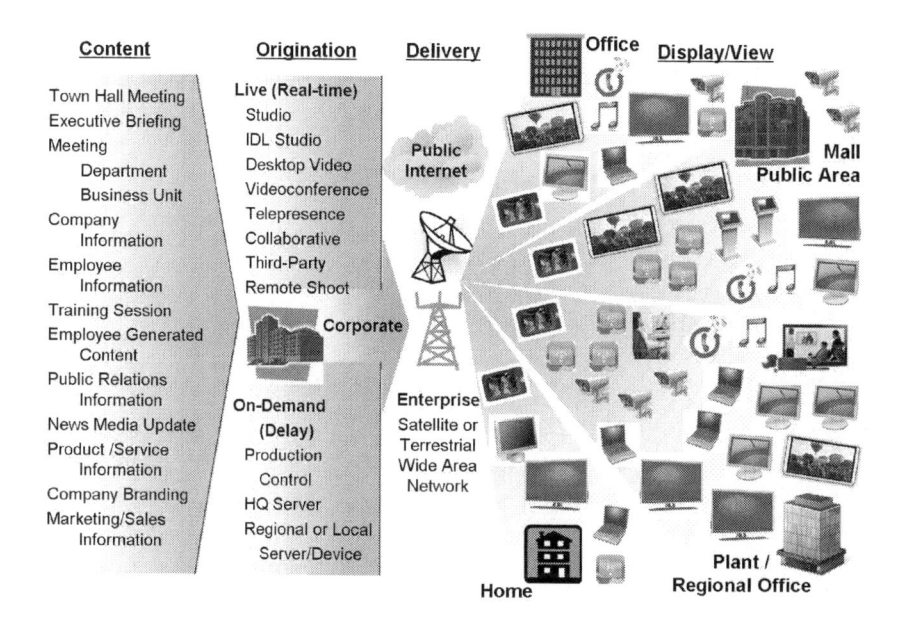

Content	Origination	Delivery	Display/View
Town Hall Meeting	Live (Real-time)		Office
Executive Briefing	Studio		
Meeting	IDL Studio	Public	Mall
Department	Desktop Video	Internet	Public Area
Business Unit	Videoconference		
Company Information	Telepresence		
Employee Information	Collaborative		
Training Session	Third-Party		
Employee Generated Content	Remote Shoot	Corporate	
Public Relations Information			
News Media Update	On-Demand	Enterprise	
Product /Service Information	(Delay)	Satellite or Terrestrial	
Company Branding	Production Control	Wide Area Network	
Marketing/Sales Information	HQ Server		
	Regional or Local Server/Device		Home / Plant / Regional Office

Digital Touch Points

Companies have the option to purchase and build home-grown solutions or follow the industry trend to purchase systems and services through one or more industry integrators as Managed Video as a Service (MVaaS). All approaches are viable and should be based on a company's procurement practice. However, what is critical is that the solution be based on a well-thought out strategy, which is inclusive of all users, targeted audiences, distribution channels, etc.

It should be noted that cameras, recording devices, content management systems, facial recognition and analytics solutions for loss prevention and video surveillance are similar to those used in communications and training.

Implement a Hybrid Content Delivery Network

The previous section covers the use of numerous inter-changeable parts in a company's entire video ecosystem. This section will address the distribution channels used to deliver content from one or more locations to the targeted viewing locations, e.g.:

- Wide area network (WAN);
- Local area network (LAN);
- Internal television and digital signage networks;
- Public Internet and Cloud services.

Also, it will cover the various applications (uses) which can be traversed over the respective channels.

The term *hybrid* is to suggest that a combination of terrestrial, satellite, and wireless networks should be embraced, to achieve the best results as applicable for each unique communications application. The actual mix of channels will vary from company to company, due to the corporate model. The following questions help identify the most viable delivery approach:

Blend Digital Media Channels

- ➢ Where does the company have a presence? Regional, continental U.S., global?
- ➢ What is the company size?
  - How many locations?
  Retail, service and hospitality businesses will have more (customer facing) locations vs. manufacturing companies.
  - How many employees and what is their work environment?
  Desktops and licensing for individual viewing will be different than group viewing.
- ➢ What are the facility types and locations? Delivery channels will be impacted if they are:
  - Store and branch offices vs. high-rise buildings and manufacturing plants;
  - Anchor and strip malls vs. self-standing facilities;
  - Metropolitan vs. rural areas.
- ➢ What is the company culture? Video and media centric companies encourage the use of social media.
  - Is it driven by customer service - the customer experience?
  - Is it training and learning oriented?
  - Is it meeting-centric?
  - Are executives visible and engaging?
- ➢ What is the existing infrastructure and what are the system capabilities?
  - What video and media tools and distribution channels are utilized?
  - Where do the company's media assets reside?
  - What are the back-up systems and capabilities?
  - What capabilities are known to be lacking?
  - Where are the current equipment and systems in their life-cycle?

There are a few assumptions and determinations which may be derived from how a company applies the above-listed criteria:

- Retail and service businesses will require a strategy for visibility to consumers that leverage the Internet to increase touch points;
- Senior executives should be engaged with employees and available to the news media and financial markets;
- Video and media-centric companies already have many of the systems included in the video ecosystem and existing distribution channels;
- Companies with numerous and rural or remote locations may have existing satellite networks to leverage;
- Companies with numerous, distant/global locations and the need to reach people on mobile devices require a hybrid of delivery approaches.

In addition to the public Internet, with its social media and video sharing channels and enterprise-wide collaborative tools, there are viable video systems and media channels which drive, complement and supplement corporate communications. As mentioned earlier, this includes satellite-based networks, live and on-demand interactive distance learning (IDL) systems, two-way videoconference and telepresence systems, webcasting and streaming media, digital signage and mobile interactive devices. However, the most significant piece in the entire ecosystem may be the Cloud, as companies and vendors are learning how best to leverage its flexibility, robustness and potential efficiencies.

Following are a few high-level system descriptions. The intent is to show how successful companies are blending terrestrial and satellite delivery channels.

Business Television (BTV) and Video Networks

Business television networks (BTV) are commonly referred to as satellite-based networks. However, the more general description goes back decades and applies to all channels used to deliver content throughout a company. This can include

Blend Digital Media Channels

live broadcasts or multicasts over the satellite network, as well as terrestrial networks. Depending on the company's capabilities and perspective, it can include videoconferences or telepresence.

Also, BTV networks are used to deliver content for delayed or on-demand viewing, where the content is stored on tape machines, edge devices (like DVRs and set-top boxes, servers, etc.) or computers. The BTV term can be applied to a less technical network: the "sneaker net", where the content is delivered on removable media such as DVDs, flash drives and even VHS videotape.

Programming originates from the company's production studio, distance learning studio, or any system with a camera and encoder/transmission capability, including computers (e.g.: Skype). Content is viewed on large screens for group viewing or individual workstations or mobile devices.

> **JC Penney Company** has long-maintained a satellite-based video network to provide training and communications to store managers and employees at its 1,200 store locations as well as the news media and financial markets.
>
> JCP delivers content to display screens in training rooms for group viewing and extends the network reach to large display screens in break rooms for corporate information and other digital signage applications.
>
> The network features interactive distance learning (IDL) functionality, where employees interact with the instructor via audio and text and take tests using iPads as the keypad and control device. In addition, the iPads perform as a viewing device to allow employees access to content while on the sales floor.
>
> **Safeway Inc.** uses numerous networks to deliver employee information and training for live and on-demand viewing to large display screens in break rooms,

Digital Touch Points

store manager desktops, and digital signage screens at select areas in stores.

The Safeway satellite network distributes content to its 1,725 store locations and includes keypads to provide interactive distance learning functionality.

In addition, Safeway uses a number of other delivery solutions to provide live and on-demand viewing of training and information over its corporate terrestrial network. The company's media production group is responsible for all video content, including Safeway videos on public and commercial YouTube Internet sites.

Government Educational Television Network (GETN) is a network of 10 Federal Government agencies that uses a common satellite carrier to share distance learning content and facilities. GETN includes such agencies as the US Air Force, Air National Guard, US Army, US Navy, FAA, Department of Justice and National Park Service. GETN had its start in 1993 with two uplinks and has grown to four uplinks reaching over 1,400 downlink locations throughout the Continental US (CONUS), Alaska, Hawaii, and Puerto Rico.

The Air Technology Network Program Management Office (ATN PMO), for example, located at Wright-Patterson AFB, OH, performs as a key hub facility for the Department of Defense (DOD). ATN PMO transmits original programming from its broadcast center and 21 additional broadcast centers of other agencies, which are located throughout the country, via terrestrial T-1 lines. ATN PMO also shares programming with non-GETN government agencies such as the Veterans Administration and broadcasts content to military bases located overseas.

The GETN network demonstrates the effectiveness of satellite to emulate the classroom by conducting live, interactive instruction to classroom viewing

Blend Digital Media Channels

environments at a distance. The classroom setting is more conducive to learning for longer courses by avoiding the distractions of the office environment. All of the GETN agencies have upgraded their classroom systems to high-definition TV and some have added a satellite delivery capability to reach desktops for short video courses either live of on-demand.

GETN distance learning instructors find that student performance is at least equal to residence classes. They also find that costs for satellite transmissions, audio interaction, system maintenance and personnel are approximately 10 percent of residence instruction.

The cost per student-hour for in-residence training averages $45 (including only travel and per diem costs), whereas the cost per student-hour via satellite is only $4.[18]

The GETN network provides an excellent example of how different groups with common objectives can blend their resources to reach targeted audiences and share content. This model can apply to companies with multiple departments and geographically dispersed divisions or operating companies. Although the initial infrastructure costs are not factored in the model (they are the responsibility of the individual agencies), they still provide compelling business justifications when included. GETN has successfully endured for 20 years by proving to be cost-efficient and being an effective method for learning: emulating the classroom, while extending the reach to viewers throughout the country and around the globe.

Return audio for live interaction as well as delivery confirmations, testing and polling results, network management, and system and user metrics arc typically handled over the enterprise terrestrial network.

---

[18] Dr. Philip Westfall, *The Government Education & Training Network (GETN): making HDTV and IPTV cost-effective options for distance learning.* (Presentation) Society for Applied Learning Technology (SALT) Conference (August 2013).

Digital Touch Points

Public Internet and Corporate Channels

The Internet is a powerful channel for companies to inform, entertain and educate consumers on products and services, rivaling the traditional broadcast and media outlets. Best-of-breed companies allocate significant resources to create and maintain their corporate websites. The most compelling websites feature video and rich media to enhance the brand and the customer experience surpassing text and basic brochure-ware information.

Many companies leverage webhosting sites such as YouTube and Vimeo to provide corporate managed channels. They use the sites to share brand information and distribute unique marketing campaigns in the hopes they go viral. Consumer product and retail companies are some of the most prolific users, including: automotive companies, retail chains, grocery stores and box stores, soft drink companies and quick service restaurants.

The role and value of advertising agencies and public relations firms can be critical to the success of online advertisements, video placements and strategically targeted product announcements and news stories. Often, the use of online video is well-integrated into a company's media strategy and complements, or even introduces, traditional marketing broadcast and print campaigns. Successful companies are finding ways to integrate the efforts of outside agencies with internal departments to ensure the content is leveraged across all viable media channels.

A few of the companies I believe successfully pioneered the use of the Internet for viral video applications are: Blendtec, BMW and Honda.

> **Blendtec** CEO Tom Dickson hosts *Will It Blend*, an ongoing series of infomercials. In the videos, Dickson demonstrates the company's products by blending a variety of items such as: cell phones, golf balls, marbles, an iPad, rake handle, miniature football helmets, CDs and DVDs. Viewers are encouraged to

Blend Digital Media Channels

submit requests for items to be blended. The *Will It Blend* campaign is credited with a significant impact on sales and has tallied around 300 million views on YouTube.

BMW released *The Hire* in 2001 - 2002 for distribution via the Internet. It was a series of high-quality short films to coincide with the introduction of new BMW vehicles. Each film featured a character called The Driver (Clive Owen) who helped people in need, showcasing his driving skills and performance aspects of the cars. The marketing campaigns were enhanced through media exposure, premiere parties, DVD giveaways, a limited-series of comic books and other novel, unique channels. BMW saw a 12% increase in sales from the previous year once the series was introduced. The films were originally posted on a BMW website, where they received over 100 million views in four years. Today, they still can be found on YouTube and other viral video websites.

Honda aired a two-minute commercial "Cog" in 2003 on British television to promote its Accord line of cars. "Cog" is a single take of car parts moving from left to right in an amazing domino chain of events to ultimately introduce an automobile. The commercial attained immediate results driving huge traffic to Honda's UK domain website and additional views through interactive television. The full version of "Cog" was broadcast a total of 10 times in the U.K. and select countries. The only way it could be viewed in the U.S. was via the Internet. The "Cog" won critical acclaim and swept most commercial awards. Honda vehicles sales in the U.K. increased by 28%, despite lower overall marketing costs. It can be found on YouTube and other viral video websites.

Digital Touch Points

Companies are integrating the use of video and rich media via the Internet, in collaboration with broadcast and print media as well as creative social media applications, to expand visibility and increase digital touch points. Companies feature commercials, infomercials and entertainment videos as well as feel good stories about community activities, employees and customers and provide tie-ins to non-profit organizations.

> **PespiCo, Inc.** introduced its first "Crash the Super Bowl" commercial campaign for Super Bowl XLI in February 2007. Consumers were invited to submit 30 second commercials for Doritos, the snack food made by its Frito-Lay division. The online campaign was conducted on the Yahoo! Video site, where contestants used tools from Yahoo to create and upload their videos.[19] Five commercials were chosen as finalists from the 1,065 entries.[20] They were posted on Yahoo, where more than one million people voted for their favorite spot.
>
> According to the International Public Relations Association (IPRA), the competition led to a 12% increase in sales of Doritos in January. In the months following the Super Bowl, PepsiCo broadcast all five commercials that had made the "Crash the Super Bowl" finals, including the winning spot *Live the Flavor*.[21]
>
> The "Crash the Super Bowl" commercial campaign was again used for the 2009 Super Bowl and every Super Bowl since. PepsiCo now combines online, offline and mobile elements with traditional media placements, which are scheduled before, during and after the Super Bowl.[22]

The success of PepsiCo's "Crash the Super Bowl" campaign influenced other companies to attempt online contests and activities for Super Bowls, based on user-generated content or

---

[19] Paul R. La Monica, *Doritos: You create our Super Bowl commercial* CNNMoney.com (September 2006).
[20] Dan L., *A brief history of the Crash the Super Bowl Contest* VideoContestNews.com (January 2012).
[21] *Doritos Crashes the Superbowl* IPRA Press Release 2007
[22] Lisa Arthur, *Three Lessons from Pepsi's Super Bowl XLV Ad Campaign* Forbes.com (February 2011).

voting, including Chevrolet, CareerBuilder, Coca-Cola and the National Football League (NFL).[23]

> **Kmart** posted a commercial in 2013 on its Facebook page to promote its free shipping service. The video features a variety of in-store shoppers who state they will *ship their pants* but in a way that creatively captures viewers' attention. The ad received immediate and extensive coverage by the news media and was shared via social media and across video webhosting sites. Kmart followed up with a *Big Gas Savings* online campaign where customers at Kmart gas pumps touted their big gas savings.

> **Macy's** saluted American Icons through the summer of 2013, including legendary fashion designers, baseball, drive-in movies, landscapes, people, traditions and veterans. *Macy's Great American Road Trip* featured company spokespersons Megan and Liz on a road trip that ended at the New York Macy's on the 4th of July. Macy's customers and fans followed Megan and Liz on the company's macys.com/icons website, where they could purchase American Icons products. The promotion coincided with Macy's support of the "Got Your 6" campaign to assist America's millions of military veterans as they return home in six key areas: jobs, education, health, housing, family and leadership. Macy's campaigns received extensive sharing across multiple social media and hosted websites.

Public websites and social media can again be a bit like the "Wild West" where it is difficult for a company to manage or control content when it can be submitted by anyone. There are a number of branding blunders where unauthorized content found an audience via the Internet. A couple of the more notable ones are:

---

[23] E.J. Schultz, *Why 'Crash the Super Bowl' Hasn't Burned Out for Doritos* Adage.com (January 2013).

Digital Touch Points

United Airlines damaged a passenger's guitar during a 2008 flight. Following nine months of failed attempts to have the airline provide compensation, Dave Carroll posted a series of videos on YouTube: songs he recorded about the incident called "United Breaks Guitars." The first song was an immediate success garnering 5 million hits within a month. Carroll refused United's compensation offer, which came within 24 hours of the first song's posting. Also, he wrote a book about the experience, became a speaker on customer service, and advanced his musical career. United apologized for the incident, donated $3,000 as a gesture of goodwill, and pays Carroll royalties to use the music videos for internal customer service training.

Domino's Pizza experienced a barrage of bad publicity and media exposure in 2009 when two employees of a local franchise recorded their tasteless tampering of food and posted it on YouTube. Discussions of Domino's and the video spread throughout the Twitter universe. Domino's responded via a Twitter account and with a video message from the CEO which was posted on YouTube.

Taco Bell, Wendy's and other quick service restaurant companies have experienced similar incidents where employees populated social media sites with videos featuring acts of poor judgment.

These are the type of digital touch points companies need to avoid.

Digital Signage

Although the term digital signage may best reference the technology (e.g.: digital screens, display systems, LCD, LED and OLED displays, etc.) used to display video and other visual media, it is generally accepted to represent the electronic display of information. Although digital signage is the next generation replacing the analog televisions many company's

used (since the 1970s) to display content in public areas, today, it is often referred to by other names:
- Digital Media Networks (Systems);
- DOOH – Digital Out of Home;
- Captive Audience Networks;
- Digital Briefing Boards;
- Electronic (E-) Billboards.

Discussions on digital signage typically fall into two distinct camps, based on content type or application:
1. Revenue generation-based advertising, marketing and promotions;
2. Enterprise communications for information and training.

Many of the technologies, software, distribution methods, management systems and measurement methodologies are the same or very similar for both applications.

It is very common to find display screens in building lobbies, public meeting spaces and cafeterias and other high-traffic areas. Information and programming content is provided for employees, guests and customers. The content varies widely, including: text, high-end graphics, live news and information from third-party commercial program services, RSS feeds for news, financial, and weather; and video clips and programs produced by the company. This may include content delivered over the company's BTV network channels.

Typically, screens are segmented into zones, featuring video and/or information from distinct sources (channels). In the event of emergency situations or system-wide alerts (on any level: local, regional, national, global), life-safety messages over-ride the system to initiate immediate action.

Companies develop content playlists through their digital signage system, in a manner very similar to how radio and television stations program their broadcast schedules. The playlist is programmed to designate content type and source to be displayed in each zone and establish the duration of play for

Digital Touch Points

each content element. Playlist metadata may provide additional information such as content owner, frequency of display, run duration (e.g.: end of content life – removal date/time) and day-parting schedules. This is to establish the best time of day to display specific content for unique viewing locations and targeted audiences.

In many cases, multiple screens are located in specific areas, featuring unique content that is differentiated by presentation modes. For example, portrait (vertical) screens may display meeting schedules and wayfinding information. Landscape (horizontal) screens may display videos and other organizational content.

> **The World Bank Group (Bank)** – The Bank is an international organization consisting of 188 member countries. Its mission is to promote sustainable economic development and reduce poverty in developing countries. The Bank has about two-hundred meeting and conference rooms at its headquarters in Washington, D.C., where it hosts thousands of on-premise meetings each year.
>
> The Bank uses a digital signage system to provide meeting room and wayfinding information for its guests and employees at strategic locations throughout the organization's eight building complex. In addition, the screens display helpful and timely institutional messages about the Bank as well as current events and activities. Other display screens are installed in numerous departments to provide content relevant to each unique audience, including the Treasury Department, which features multiple private channels on its trading floor and two channels for public areas. The Bank leverages the ability to share content between the institutional and department digital signage systems and other media channels throughout the organization.

Companies with branch offices and store locations display product and service offerings and provide branding messages on the display screens in lobbies, merchandise departments, end-of-aisle (end-caps), at the checkout lanes, information counters and teller windows.

Cabela's Inc., a specialty retailer of hunting, fishing, camping, and related outdoor merchandise, has evolved into the world's largest mail order, retail, and Internet outdoor outfitter. Although the company has long been known to use video, producing programs on outdoor adventures for television and content for its YouTube video channel, it incorporates video and rich media into its customer and employee communications. Also, digital signage, including videowalls and endcap display screens are located on show-room floors. The endcap screens primarily display product information and the videowalls feature outdoor activities such as hunting, fly fishing and camping.

In addition, the company has large display screens in the store breakrooms to provide information targeted for associate outfitters. The network is designed to improve employee engagement by featuring topics of interest and infotainment, including recognition of associate outfitters and company benefits. The network also provides preview showings of new programs for the broadcast channels. The objective is to provide content that is not considered required or invasive of employee time and space.

Financial institutions are displaying messages, product offerings and branding in the branch lobbies, at check and information counters, at the teller windows and at the drive-thru.

Hotels are displaying products and services, hotel chain information, guest meetings and activities, local attractions and restaurants, travel guides and weather information. Some screens serve as a source of entertainment featuring artwork, video clips and personal pictures downloaded by guests.

Digital Touch Points

The content featured on digital signage systems may include:
- Product and service information;
- Company branding;
- News, weather and information;
- Community news and activities;
- Profiles of branch representatives and community members;
- Wayfinding (directions and maps);
- Life-safety notifications;
- Interactive messaging and tie-ins to company information;
- Redirection to other media, including the company's website.

Companies use digital signage to replace the use of poster boards, billboards, pamphlets and other hard copy notices which are commonly posted throughout lobbies and other public areas. Although the cost of the digital signage system is not offset by the elimination of poster boards and paper notices, the organization does benefit from the:
- Cost avoidance for creation and production of the posters;
- Time management (manual labor) savings by not having to create, place and then retrieve the posters;
- Reduction in paper clutter, resulting in a cleaner (greener) environment.

Additional benefits may include:
- Improved guest experience through:
  - Wayfinding service;
  - Perceived shortened wait times;
- Improved communications and training through time-shifting:

- Making content available for on-demand viewing, especially for employees with limited access to PCs;
- Improved employee morale by:
  - Being informed of company events and activities;
  - Creating sense of community amongst employees.

Digital signage is an excellent tool to direct customers to the company's public websites and drive employees to internal websites for detailed information on relevant topics and events.

Mobile Devices

Reaching customers and employees via mobile devices is nearly as important to the success of a company as the concept of content being king. Mobile devices are a preferred way for people to consume content all of the time and everywhere. By leveraging this trend, a company improves the ability to increase its digital touch points.

> Get content to customers and employees where they are, when they want it and on the viewing device of choice, with the ability to interact and share content.

Mayo Clinic developed a number of innovative custom apps for physicians and patients to use on the 15,000 iOS devices throughout the clinic's network. The *Synthesis Mobile* app taps into the clinic's internal systems, giving physician's instant access to information including electronic medical records (EMR) and billing data. The *Patient* app lets patients access their personal information and exchange messages with their physicians. The *Ask Mayo Expert* app provides information on medical conditions and treatments from the clinic's subject matter experts. The apps save physicians time and make them more efficient. According to Dr. Brad Leibovich, Mayo Clinic, *Synthesis Mobile* provides a "...*personal interaction between the physician and the patient.*"[24]

Digital Touch Points

Companies with field sales representatives and service technicians may use their mobile devices to show customers video clips and other media relevant to their unique situation such as pest control, home or appliance repair, insurance claims or financial planning.

> **Rollins** complements its core network and in-class training with video clips and other media for downloading to mobile devices. Field service technicians can view content to identify the cause of problems or gain insight on how to treat and control pest related issues.
>
> Also, the technicians are provided software programs on the same mobile devices to create quotes and invoices, provide protection information, and draw floor plans and images of the home or facility highlighting areas of pest problems.
>
> The objective is to provide the company representatives with the tools to perform their jobs. Rollins expects to see improved efficiencies and an increase in customer satisfaction and revenues.

Successful companies are enabling their field representatives to take pictures, record video or send live feeds of occurrences or circumstances back to headquarters for immediate response and guidance.

In-branch and in-store retail service and sales representatives may use their mobile devices to view information or participate in a training session during customer-facing downtime. Visit an Apple store for a first-class experience.

As covered in other sections, customers can interact with in-store digital signage systems and kiosks while also conducting on-line research or other activities.

> **Lowe's**, a home improvement retailer, is a good example as it implemented a number technology upgrades to "handle video downloads for employee selling tools and customer Wi-Fi usage,"[25] according to

---

[24] 'A Medical Leader Brings New Innovations to Patient Care with Apps for iPhone, iPad, and iPad Mini' Apple.com (2013).

Robert Niblock, Lowe's CEO. In addition, Lowes provided mobile devices to store employees so they can better serve customers and "enable the ability to tender a sale at any place in the store."

Customers at locations with digital signage systems are using their mobile devices to dial into numbers posted on screen. They will receive unique content, which is downloaded to their device, where they can respond to surveys and other actionable requests. Information, including alerts and emergency notifications, can be directed to all digital signage screens throughout the network and mobile devices.

Bleeding edge companies have integrated mobile devices into their training and communication networks to function as interactive tools for audio interaction, polling, testing and surveys. It is anticipated that numerous companies will embrace this as a best practice implementation.

Surveillance Systems
Enhance Applications and Value

Video surveillance systems have become a critical tool for companies to provide personal and property security and improve loss prevention (LP). Security cameras are virtually everywhere: in retail and service branches, sales floors, building interiors, exteriors and parking lots, street intersections, along highways and busy streets, inside public transit vehicles, etc.

Surveillance systems can be on-premise or integrated into a company's entire network infrastructure to allow centralized management and control.

The systems can deter or decrease theft and criminal activities or assist in capturing the perpetrator(s). Although this may not be a favorable digital touch point action, this video application clearly contributes to a company's bottom line by reducing

---

[25] Chris Murphy, *From Lowe's to Coke, 8 CEOs Talk Tech Strategy* (April 9, 2012) InformationWeek.com (2012).

losses, managing insurance costs and limiting exposure to litigation.

Security systems can be invaluable for unexpected situations, such as the well documented 2013 Boston Marathon bombing and the 2011 Tucson shooting of U.S. Representative Gabrielle Giffords and 18 other people. Video from a local retail store's security system contributed to the identification of the bombing suspects. Video from the security system of the supermarket where the Gifford campaign meeting was being conducted documented many of the events around the shooting spree.

The Cloud – Cloud Services

The Cloud is addressed in the latter part of this section purposely. It allows the descriptions and examples of systems and capabilities familiar to most individuals and used by many companies to set the playing field. Also, the role and value of the Cloud to companies is yet to be fully established.

It is somewhat ironic that the Cloud may offer the most upside for companies than any other element of the video ecosystem, while also presenting the largest conundrum.

It may be helpful to first clarify the difference between the Cloud and the Internet. The Internet is a giant network of unmanaged networks which provides access to the web. Essentially, the Internet is a tool, not a service. The Cloud, on-the-other-hand, can be defined in many ways, but for the purpose of this book, it will be referred to as a cloud service. As a cloud service, it is a managed resource where a vendor[26] provides the infrastructure and 24/7 support that enables companies to implement applications over the Internet or private networks.[27] The primary benefits of cloud services is that it provides a company the way to increase capacity or add capabilities quickly without the need to research solutions and vendors, invest in new infrastructure, licensing of software and training of personnel.

---

[26] Webopedia.com
[27] Gerben Meijer, *"The Cloud" vs The Internet* cloud provider usa.com (October 2012).

The alternative to cloud service is for companies to buy and self-manage the servers or rent them from a third-party vendor. In this scenario, companies must also work with an Internet service provider (ISP) and/or content delivery network (CDN).

> **Internet** - A giant network of unmanaged networks which provides access to the web. It is a tool, not a service.
>
> **Cloud** - A managed resource where a vendor provides the infrastructure and 24/7 support that enables companies to implement applications over the Internet or private networks.
>
> **Cloud Provider** - A service provider that offers customers storage or software services available via a private (private cloud) or public network (cloud). Usually, it means the storage and software are available for access via the Internet.

To manage a company's video and media content via the Cloud, a service provider could be a video systems integrator or network services company.

There are a number of key issues a company needs to address when selecting its approach to using cloud services:

- ➢ How much video and dynamic media content will the company produce and provide?
  - o To internal and external audiences?
  - o Live or on-demand?
- ➢ What media types will be maintained in the Cloud?
- ➢ How will viewers access the content?
- ➢ What content search functionality is needed?
- ➢ What viewer functionality is needed for feedback and interaction?

Digital Touch Points

- ➤ What tracking and measurement functionality is needed – Analytics?
- ➤ What is the anticipated consumption rate of the content?

The primary objective is to ensure that the content is readily available and easily accessible to the targeted viewer(s). However, it is important to recognize that the abundance of technology and approaches create the need for well-thought-out selection, implementation and ongoing operation plans, which should consider:

- ➤ What is the current workflow?
- ➤ How will the workflow change with cloud services?
  - ○ Who provides the content?
  - ○ Who is responsible for metadata information?
    - Establishing naming conventions and criteria?
    - Inputting the metadata?
    - Managing the ongoing effectiveness of the metadata program?
  - ○ Who is responsible for content oversight – protection of the corporate brand?
  - ○ Who has administrative control of the content?
  - ○ Who has access to the content and authorization to use and modify?
- ➤ What is the life expectancy of the content?
  - ○ How often will the content be made available?
  - ○ Will it have a pre-determined end-of-life?
  - ○ Will it be seasonal or have additional uses for availability?

Companies must clearly identify the difference between active content and content which can be stored or archived. Also, they must recognize the difference between finished pieces versus raw footage or content that is re-purposed for additional uses.

Although the Cloud can provide quick and easy access to content which is active, it is not likely to be cost effective as a storage device for content that is outdated or not needed in the foreseeable future. Also, the company should determine whether in-house servers or the Cloud are the best approach to back-up video content. Refer to Chapter 8 on preserving and protecting media assets.

Staffing Resources Go Media-Centric!
Allocate Experienced Staff to Manage Video Content and Media Assets

Gone are the days where the video department was responsible for all things video: where content was shot, edited, distributed, displayed and funded by the video group. Today, it is common for numerous departments to produce video content, whether it be corporate sanctioned or informal. Informal content is another term for employee generated content (UGC), where anyone may produce and desire to distribute a story or topic of interest via the company's communication channels.

Essentially, the way a company manages video content in today's media-centric environment can prove to be opportunistic and invaluable to the company or create embarrassing or damaging incidents if allowed to perform outside of corporate governance.

A company needs to ensure that it has the right staffing resources to produce and/or manage the distribution of corporate and affiliated information. This requires sufficient head count and the individuals should have the right skills. In some companies, this may require a sea-change, where video production and audiovisual specialists and engineers need to be balanced with media specialists and computer/data-centric expertise. Where possible, it can be done through employee training and acquiring industry certifications. Otherwise, qualified resources may need to be hired or engaged through a staffing resource provider.

As the use of video rampages through the company, it is advisable to have adequate resources to approve and manage the informally produced content. The cost for the headcount can be mitigated over time, if the appropriate policies and processes are implemented up front to avoid timely and costly oversights.

Business Drivers of Blended Communications
With Benefits

Blended communications helps organizations:
- Leverage existing facilities, tools and resources;
- Embrace new media;
- Efficiently and effectively communicate throughout the company, as well as external audiences;
- Aggregate and centralize knowledge and skills;
- Eliminate silos and compartmentalization;
- Increase workflow efficiencies;
- Support the company's business drivers;
- Reduce and/or control costs.

Other recognizable benefits of blended communications include but are not limited to:
- Increased sales;
- Enhanced brand;
- Improved employee awareness and satisfaction;
- Reduced employee turnover;
- Improved timeliness of information distribution;
- Improved customer satisfaction.

Edward Jones is one of the early companies to embrace video as a strategic tool for communications and training to achieve improved business results. The company continuously leverages the best of off-the-shelf products with customized solutions that are developed in-house. As stated by John Bachmann, Managing Partner 1980 – 2004:

Blend Digital Media Channels

"A company can't win with technology, but it can be beaten without it!"

Tips and Perspectives

- Develop a media business strategy as the foundation to develop the communications strategy and implementation plan.
- Establish collaboration across user and functional support groups.
- Develop a communication strategy and business plan to select and implement the right systems and workflow.

  Leverage existing media channels and resources;

  Implement an enterprise-wide solution;

  Consider a hybrid solution of delivery channels;

  Allocate funding responsibility to appropriate parties;

  Allocate headcount and train staffing resources.

- When evaluating and implementing systems, ensure that they integrate with all other components of the company's video ecosystem.

  Solutions will be more affordable and robust than years past.

  Staffing costs may exceed solution implementations, especially at the outset.

- Distribute content using hybrid media channels - Whether terrestrial, wireless or satellite, delivery can be affordable, available and reliable.
- Leverage the Cloud and cloud services where and how they make sense:

  As an independent media channel and/or extension of other corporate channels.

Digital Touch Points

- Get the content to screens of all sizes:

   Large screens in training and conference rooms, retail floors or other common areas (e.g.: digital signage);

   Smaller screens on desktops;

   Smallest screens on mobile devices.

- Employ the right type and blend of staffing resources – Experienced video communicators that are energetic and engaged users of dynamic media.
- Staff the right number and skill types to produce and manage video content and protect the company's brand.

Chapter 7

Analytics

Striving for Business Intelligence: Results!

We are experiencing a period of intelligence where everyone is collecting analytics, statistics, data and test results to derive conclusive business information.

Companies do this by using a variety of traditional approaches to measure their marketing via broadcast media, in-store displays and print advertising. This includes: the Nielsen and Arbitron ratings, in-store surveys, coupon redemptions and loyalty programs. In addition, companies acquire information through new media such as web analytics, interactive kiosks and in-store displays, gaze tracking technology, mobile device interaction and social media channels.

As a result, companies can identify and track customer interests and activities. They can determine which customers are making purchases. They can identify the products, services and promotions garnering interest and resulting in sales. The available information is so granular, they are able to identify the path of customer behavior and exploit the cause and correlation between digital touches and off-line activity.

Bottom line, companies are driven to enhance the customer experience, enable customer engagement and collect information.

It's All About the Numbers!
Achieving the Results!

Analytics

Measurable business results are not unique to marketing and the consumer space. Also, feedback and analytics for applications over corporate internal channels have been available for decades, including the use of video-based interactive distance learning and training networks. However, the role and value of video and dynamic media systems has increased with these applications due to technology innovation.

Companies are expanding past traditional performance and volume-based metrics to include value-based training: qualitative measurements. They are looking for direct correlations between training and sales results, where product knowledge and customer service training can have a measurable impact on the customer's experience. In many ways, this makes analytics for employee activities and performance as critical to companies as CPM is in the B2C space.

Key performance indicators (KPIs) should be established for the departments and groups included in the media business strategy. Each group is likely to have standard metrics and KPIs which can be applied to video and dynamic media applications. For example, marketing will be focused on criteria for external audiences such as the number of exposures generated by the digital touch points, whether online, in-store or other. This may include:

- Number of views;
- Social interactions;
- Source of visits (direct or via search or link);
- Sales conversions (online vs. in-store);
- Sales per campaign;
- Customer satisfaction;
- Cost per lead;
- Return on investment.

The list of KPIs for training and learning organizations (and human resource departments) is extensive. However, this book is concerned with those relevant to measuring the effectiveness of video and dynamic media in the training of employees. This may include the number of employees trained and the number of courses and hours required per employee training. For training conducted via one or more of the e-learning methods, the KPIs should include the number of visits, when and duration of view (completion of course?), interactions and test results. The costs to develop and present the content (on-line or via interactive distance learning systems) should be measured against in-classroom or other training methods and factored into the department's business plan. The objective is to use video and dynamic media to impact employee performance and increase positive business results. Many companies, including those cited in this book find distance learning approaches can be as effective as in-classroom training while off-setting other costs. See the GETN example (page 64).

Many communication and media departments are familiar with KPIs as an integral piece of service level agreements in contracts with equipment and service providers. However, they need to determine criteria relevant to measuring the effectiveness of video and dynamic media across all internal and external corporate media channels. The KPIs may be similar to the other groups, tracking and measuring the number, type, frequency and duration of views. They should be in support of and/or complementary to all user groups, including executives, marketing and the training and learning organizations.

> Capture and document the digital touch points. How can you judge the effort if you can't measure results?

Learning and Training

Companies have expanded their use of interactive and tracking solutions to measure if learning has transferred to the job and to evaluate on the job performance. The information feeds into corporate learning management systems (LMS) and associated databases. LMS systems, like communications and delivery channels, have evolved significantly over the past few years adding robust features and functionality. The systems incorporate consumer-influenced capabilities with the focus on enhancing the end-user experience, such as: video and rich media, interaction and sharing of content and mobile access.

In addition to the basic functionality of managing and tracking courses, student registration, learning histories and synchronizing with HR databases, today's LMS and communication systems can provide:

- Content catalogs and metadata search functionality;
- Integrated content and talent management;
- Integration with IT and company-wide systems and databases, including marketing and corporate communication media channels;
- Enhanced security;
- Collaborative and social learning;
- Mobile learning;
- Extensive analytics and reporting capabilities, including customer interactions.

To validate their value to the company, the learning and training organizations need to provide more detailed analytical information. At the very least, it should include the type of data listed in the marketing and communication sections.

Corporate Communications and Information

As companies embrace video systems and media channels to conduct meetings and training sessions and distribute corporate information, they are using robust and flexible tools and systems to track and measure audience participation. They are capturing detailed information about the content, each individual viewer's activity and participation and the performance of the network.

Analytics

The information can apply to the delivery of live and on-demand content to internal and external targeted audiences. It can include but not be limited to:

Program Content and Views:

- Programs viewed, as listed by:
  - Title, topic, category;
  - Unique viewer ID;
  - The viewer locations or sites;
  - Viewing by site or group;
  - Number of views;
  - Date viewed, completed view;
- Total number, average and maximum (per specified period) for:
  - Programs viewed;
  - Program minutes viewed;
  - Percentage of program viewed;
  - Unique program viewers;
  - Programs downloaded;
  - Viewed programs and minutes viewed per:
    - Geographic region;
    - Brands;
    - Departments;
- The number of dropped viewers per program by:
  - Unique viewer ID;
  - Time mark and duration;

Program Participation and Interaction:

- Presenter provided questions;
- Viewer questions to Presenter or Subject Matter Expert (SME);
- Chats and messaging amongst viewers;
- Polls and surveys.

The communications and video departments, as well as the learning and training groups, need to utilize as much as possible, the tools and means used by the marketing

Digital Touch Points

organizations to track, evaluate and measure digital touch points and results.

> Implement the systems to validate results –
> Return on Investment!

Tips and Perspectives

- Have the right systems to manage data across the enterprise.
- Get the full engagement and support from the IT group: *To ensure the systems are fully integrated.*
- Capture analytics for each functional area that uses video and dynamic media including:
    o Marketing;
    o Training;
    o Communications.
- Allocate the staffing resources to manage, evaluate and interpret the data.
- Ensure that the staff is properly trained to mine the data for usable information and business intelligence: *What good is the data if you do not know how to interpret it?*
- Distribute the analytics to all executives and responsible parties.
- Derive actionable intelligence and take action – Don't miss opportunities!
- Govern the ongoing use of the data to ensure improved business results.

Chapter 8

Protect Company Media Assets

Of the 5,000 U.S. publicly traded companies, nearly one-tenth of them have celebrated their centennial anniversaries.[28] It is fair to assume that they have extensive collections of documents, pictures, film, videotape and other memorabilia of their long and storied histories.

Some best-of-breed companies have invested time and resources to catalog and archive these media assets. Although it may have been a time-consuming and tedious process, they are able to utilize the media featuring cherished and relevant content in corporate programs, orientation videos, commercials, news stories, publications and presentations. Most important, these companies have preserved and protected their historical content, which can be invaluable for generations to come.

In addition, and as addressed earlier, employees throughout the company are recording content of all types and subjects, on consumer cameras, phones and devices as well as through their corporate media service organizations. For some companies the amount of new content is overwhelming. It is creating new challenges requiring resources, systems and processes to manage how and where the content is used and to protect the corporate brand.

Digital Workflow – DAMs & MAMs

Today's technologies allow all companies, regardless of age and size, the ability to capture and retain key and sensitive moments about their people, facilities, products, services and success stories. Successful companies are implementing digital asset management (DAM) and media asset management (MAM) systems into their video and media ecosystems. Also, they are introducing digital workflow processes to ensure efficient and effective use of their media assets.

---

[28] *USA Today* (July 2011), analysis by Standard & Poor's Capital IQ

Digital Touch Points

DAMs and MAMs have been around for years, serving the broadcast and publishing industries, and now, due to the widespread use of media, are embraced in the enterprise market. It should be noted that there is a difference between DAMs and MAMs, which can be significant for video and media-centric companies.

> **Digital Asset Management Systems (DAMS)** include computer software and hardware systems that help manage digital assets, which are typically associated with static media such as: images, word documents, PDFs, etc. Digital content is stored in databases called asset repositories while metadata are stored in separate databases called media catalogs and are pointed to the original items.
>
> **Media Asset Management Systems (MAMS)** are a sub-category of DAM systems and mainly manage video and audio assets (e.g.: interviews, news clips and training modules). To a lesser degree, MAMS also manage other media such as: animations, digital photos and music as well as word documents, PDFs and images.

Also, there are different types of asset management systems relevant to video and media.[29]

---

[29] *What is a Digital Asset Management System (DAM)?* Contentmanager.eu.com

Protect Company Media Assets

> **Common Types of Digital Asset Management Systems**
>
> **Brand** - Emphasis is on the facilitation of content re-use within large organizations, where the content is largely marketing or sales related, such as: product imagery, logos and marketing collateral.
>
> **Library** - Emphasis is on storage and retrieval of large amounts of infrequently changing media assets, such as: video, music and photographs.
>
> **Production** - Emphasis is on managing assets as they are created for a digital media production, such as: video clips, animation, music and visual-effects. They usually include work-flow and project-management features coupled with the storage, organization and revision control of frequently changing digital assets.

A DAM provides a number of functions which may include:

- Organizing digital assets;
- Manipulating the assets:
  - Converting, merging and collating;
- Searching for assets;
- Verifying the integrity of the assets;
- Delivery and distribution of the assets;
- Securing the assets, which may include copyright protection;
- Backing up the assets.

One of the biggest areas of confusion about a DAM is the storing of content. What does this really mean?

As mentioned in Chapter 6, companies should clearly identify the difference between active content and content which can be

Digital Touch Points

stored or archived. Also, they should recognize the difference between finished pieces versus raw footage or content that is re-purposed for additional uses.

It is important to understand the difference between storing the content in an active system and storing it in archival state or a backup system. An active system may best be described as where content is readily available and easily accessible, whether it be for public or widespread consumption or production purposes. Backup systems provide protection in the event of instances or failures of the active systems, e.g.: disaster recovery. Based on a company's backup system and strategy, the content may be available immediately or with minimal inconvenience to the user. Archive systems are for long-term preservation and protection, where the assets are moved to off-line storage.

In addition to having a DAM system, companies need to implement a digital workflow that is unique to its media operation. Digital workflow is a process that covers the creation or production of content, acquires it, modifies or distributes the assets and supports the metadata throughout the entire video and media ecosystem. Workflows can involve numerous versions of video content which may be in different locations, in different file formats and distributed over different media channels. Metadata information is created and used to improve efficiencies toward the cataloging, searching and retrieving of content assets.

Metadata

Metadata is the description of an asset. Essentially, it is "data about data". It can vary significantly depending on the needs of the organization, user, system designer or content owner.

> **Metadata** is the description of an asset. It means "data about data". It can vary significantly depending on the needs of the organization, user, system designer or content owner. Metadata may include: captions, key words, names of producers, shooters or on-camera talent, products, locations, contact names, the means of encoding/decoding, ownership, rights of access, file names or low-resolution images.

There are different types of metadata that serve different functions. The two most basic types are technical and descriptive.

Technical metadata is data that describes the media file such as: file size, bit rate of the file, resolution, and capture device, settings and date. Much of it is automatically recorded at the time of capture and stored in the file itself.

Descriptive metadata describes the file or asset and provides the "who, what, when, where, and what is it about" information. This information is generally input manually and is then maintained in a management system.

Descriptive metadata can consist of a variety of different elements and naming conventions. However, the Dublin Core Metadata Element Set (DCMES) contains 15 commonly used elements.[30]

---

[30] *Dublin Core Metadata Element Set (DCMES)*, Dublincore.org

Digital Touch Points

Dublin Core Media Element Set

Contributor	The entity (person, department, company, etc.) responsible for making contributions to the asset.
Coverage	The location and/or time period that is relevant to the asset.
Creator	The entity (person, department, company, etc.) responsible for creating the asset.
Date	The date or period of time associated with the asset.
Description	Detailed information about the asset.
Format	The file format, physical medium, or dimensions of the asset.
Identifier	A unique reference to the asset.
Language	The language of the asset.
Publisher	The entity (person, department, company, etc.) responsible for making the asset available.
Relation	A related asset.
Rights	Information about who has the rights to the asset.
Source	A related asset from which the asset is derived.
Subject	The topic of the asset.
Title	A name given to the asset.
Type	The nature or genre of the asset.

Although the DAM solutions may be affordable, companies need staffing resources to create, input and manage the metadata information as well as to manage the and fulfill the video workflow process. Many of the responsibilities are similar to those covered in the Cloud section, including but not limited to:

- How will the workflow change with cloud services?
    - Who provides the content?
    - Who is responsible for metadata information?
        - Establishing naming conventions and criteria?
        - Inputting the metadata?
        - Managing the ongoing effectiveness of the metadata program?

- Who is responsible for content oversight – protection of the corporate brand?
- Who has administrative control of the content?
- Who has access to the content and authorization to use and modify it?

➤ What is the life expectancy of the content?
- How often will the content be made available?
- Will it have a pre-determined end-of-life?
- Will it be seasonal or have additional uses for availability?

Benefits and Business Drivers:
Cost Savings and Efficiencies

Cost savings and improved efficiencies stand out as the primary business reasons to implement a DAM/MAM solution. Some companies have justified the purchase of equipment and hiring of personnel by implementing systems throughout the organization and eliminating compartmentalized operations.

Benefits of a DAM/MAM solution may include:

Cost Savings:

➤ Through improved time management across the enterprise.

➤ Digital storage is relatively affordable and requires minimal space (real estate), much less than what is needed to store tape and film libraries.

Efficiencies in workflow and content access:

➤ Ingest, tagging and management of content is standardized.

➤ Effort and time to search for content is reduced for media managers as well as end-users (targeted viewers of the content).

➤ Process to re-purpose content is improved for additional, multiple applications.

> May improve the media operation's oversight and control of user generated content (UGC) and protect the company's brand.

Historical Value

Cost savings are important, but consider the value of your company's historical media assets: film, video, pictures and press clippings of the company founder(s), executives and distinguished employees, the first corporate headquarters, manufacturing facilities, retail outlets, or branch offices, products and packaging, major events and milestones and corporate branding.

It is common for companies to showcase key moments and accomplishments of their history in the lobbies of their facilities using digital display screens. Some companies incorporate video and media extravaganzas into museum-like display environments. In today's digital world, video clips for most organizations are featured on their corporate websites, YouTube and other social media outlets.

> **The Mayo Clinic** is an excellent example of an organization which has leveraged its historical media content. The clinic has produced numerous video programs of the Mayo brothers (Charles and William) and the company's history, including *My Brother and I: The Founding of Mayo Clinic*. The videos feature content from virtually all media formats, and document the brothers' vision and philosophy. Also, Mayo Clinic shares an endless number of patient success stories. Productions are featured on digital display screens throughout its facilities and available to employees, customers and the public for viewing or purchase via the Internet.[31]

---

[31] www.mayoclinic.com

The Coca-Cola Company has taken its branding to another level, with the World of Coca-Cola, a permanent exhibit in Atlanta, GA. The World of Coca-Cola features the history, products and prominent marketing events of the company. In addition to expansive displays of Coke memorabilia and *the freestyle* beverage fountain, historical videos and interactive media stations are located throughout the facility. The company's website is a wonderful example of how to leverage media assets to tell and market its story, blending historical footage and pictures with film and video clips, television commercials and other visual content.[32]

Companies like Coca-Cola and Mayo Clinic recognized the value of media assets early on, embedding their use in the corporate culture and utilizing the assets to enhance their respective brands.

Managing Video and Dynamic Media Assets

Managing media assets is far more than protecting and using historical content. Companies are creating more video and dynamic media than ever, for internal communications, employee training, employee profiles and community programs, product demonstrations and merchandising, marketing videos, market reports, news announcements and the list goes on.

Much of the content is created for short shelf-life, such as seasonal or sale products, quarterly reports, and videos on constantly changing regulations and policies. Other content is designed for long-term use, including safety videos, corporate image and orientation programs and training courses.

The type of content and shelf-life can vary tremendously across industries and from company to company. However, there is one constant: the use of video and dynamic media is ubiquitous throughout the enterprise space. Companies have no choice but to embrace it. The choices they do have are:

    1. To what extent will video and dynamic media be utilized?

---

[32] www.us.coca-cola.com

2. How well can they manage it and make it readily available and easily accessible?

Consequences of Maintaining Status Quo?

What is the risk of not properly preserving historical media?

Simply stated, over time, media will degrade and may eventually become unusable. Movie studios and broadcast entities are known to search for film and video recordings of old movies, programs, news clips and other documented events where original and duplicated copies have been misplaced, poorly stored or damaged due to fire, weather or mishandling. The same is true of individuals and the media they use to document their personal and family experiences. And the same is true for companies.

Film and slides are vulnerable to becoming brittle and breaking. Videotape, which is an analog recording on magnetic tape, too can break or tear, but is also subject to other risks. Video and audio tapes have an average life expectancy of only 30 years. The magnetic coating degrades due to use and age, creating what is commonly called drop-outs. Content can be erased or disturbed if the cartridge is stored near metal. Each duplication version will be at a lesser quality than the original recording. Also, there are multiple tape formats which have come and gone over the years, resulting in a diminishing number of machines available to playback the recordings. All media are subject to heat and mishandling.

Following are a number of tips and recommendations to help you through the process.

Tips and Recommendations

1. Develop a Media Asset Strategy

Thoroughly analyze the state of your company's current situation, including the ability and capabilities of equipment and systems to create, manage, deliver and display content. Establish workflow processes to create

Protect Company Media Assets

and/or approve content and approve content contributors. Identify stakeholders responsible for creating, approving, delivering and tracking content. Identify the targeted audiences, including their viewing environments and display screens for accessing and displaying the content.

It is critical to identify how a DAM and/or MAM can help the company meet its business requirements and impact the bottom line. Also, address:

- What are your current business processes?
- What is your organizational structure?
- What is the current workflow?
- How are responsibilities allocated?
- Who owns the content?
- How will you store and manage active content?
- How will you archive content for long term preservation and protection?
- Factor in back-up systems and processes.
- Do not assume everyone knows what a DAM is, why it is needed, how to select one or how to implement or manage it.
- Assign administrators to manage the system and sub-administrators to manage their own content.
- Assign a position, or establish the role for someone, to input and manage metadata, e.g.: a librarian.
- Consider legal issues, including digital rights management (DRM), compliance and risk management.
- Establish policies and share guidelines.
- Benchmark with other organizations.

- Let needs, not technology, drive the solution selection process.
- Always remember that content is king.

2. Metadata

- Defining terminology and structure of metadata is extremely important. Start with the Dublin Core Media Element Set.
- Compile as much data as possible and as early as possible, including all assets such as: scripts, prompter copy, voice-over recordings, raw footage, etc.
- Establish naming conventions and proper tagging (e.g.: include the name of the person inputting information vs. initials or nicknames, etc.).

3. Analytics

- Standardize reporting templates and functions.
- Analytics can be invaluable as long as there is a purpose.
- What is the cost if you do not embrace analytics?
- It is not just the analytics. It is the interpretation of the information.

4. Workflow

An efficient workflow is imperative to keeping track of assets. The DAM solution should be configured to help organize, track and share assets. It should be robust and flexible.

We have progressed to a highly digital environment which provides media and tools far more advanced than film and magnetic tape. However, it is critical to remember that there will be an ongoing and endless migration to new and different media formats. Do not fall victim to format obsolescence. For example, think: beta, VHS, and ¾" videotape, reel-to-reel audiotape, 4-track and 8-track audio cartridges and the audio cassette, the laserdisc, floppy disc and diskettes. Looking ahead, what is the future of the compact disc (CD), digital versatile disc (DVD, formerly digital video disc), Blu-Ray disc (BD), hard disk drives, memory cards and sticks, USB flash drive (universal serial bus) and other external, mobile hard drives?

> Do not fall victim to format obsolescence.

Move your company's media assets to digital formats where the content can be archived and protected, while being readily accessible and searchable and able to be migrated to other formats efficiently.

Digital Touch Points

Chapter 9

Managed Video as a Service (MVaaS)

Technologies and how they are used are not the only things improving. As media evolve and new technologies are implemented, the way to purchase solutions and services are also changing.

> ....As the present now will later be past
> The order is rapidly fadin'
> And the first one now will later be last
> For the times they are a-changin'.[33]
>
> Bob Dylan

Managed services have been around for decades: since Electronic Data Systems (now HP Enterprise Services) was founded in 1962 as an outsourcing resource for technology services. Now managed services is gaining traction throughout the video industry as the use of media increases and systems and operations are integrated with IT infrastructure. This is called Managed Video as a Service (MVaaS) where a vendor contractually assumes responsibility to provide equipment, software, system design and integration, (possibly) staffing resources and specified support services.

MVaaS is ideal for companies that develop a media business strategy and implement solutions with consideration toward the entire video ecosystem, from content creation and management to delivery, display and performance analytics.

Key advantages of the MVaaS approach are the reduction in up-front capital expenditures and established fixed, predictable pricing over extended periods. Other business drivers and benefits may include: the mitigation of risks to clients by avoiding obsolescence to equipment and software and future-proofing for upgrades and enhancements of new and innovative technology.

---

[33] Bob Dylan, *The Times They Are A-Changin'* (1964).

Digital Touch Points

MVaaS Services

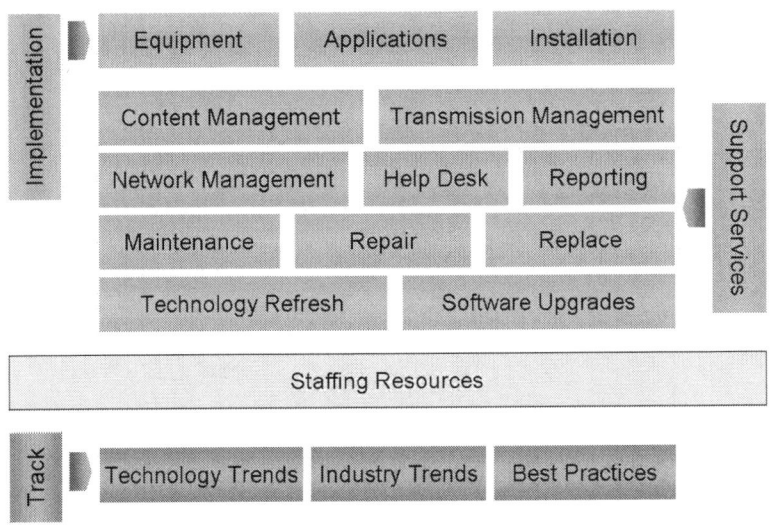

Implementation			Support Services
	Equipment	Applications	Installation	
	Content Management	Transmission Management	
	Network Management	Help Desk	Reporting	
	Maintenance	Repair	Replace	
	Technology Refresh	Software Upgrades	

Staffing Resources

Track: Technology Trends | Industry Trends | Best Practices

JC Penney Company uses MVaaS to cover most of its video network equipment including transmission and encryption systems, the store video appliances, IDL solution and keypads and mobile devices and display screens for training, communications and digital signage applications. Also, MVaaS is inclusive of specific help-desk, installation, and field support services. JCP employs all staffing resources.

Purchasing the equipment and support services as MVaaS allows JCP to operate against fixed, budgeted costs and rely on the vendor to manage technology upgrades and ensure the system maintains high performance standards.

Safeway Inc. uses MVaaS for transmission and encryption equipment, software, satellite bandwidth, IDL solution and keypads, on-premise playback devices, and the large screen displays. In addition, the MVaaS program covers help-desk, installation, and field support services. Safeway maintains all on-site staffing responsibilities.

Managed Video as a Service

The MVaaS approach allows Safeway to upgrade its network and enhance its communications with the best available technologies and display screens without having to deal with equipment or software obsolescence.

MVaaS vs. Home-grown

The beauty of MVaaS is that it can be applied to purchases and services in the manner that best suits a company's business needs. In lieu of the purchase, build-out, self-management and operation of a home-grown approach, MVaaS can be purchased in whole or with elements of home-grown.

A good way to envision the various approaches is to use a metaphor of transportation options.[34] The home-grown approach is similar to owning your personal car, where you have the freedom to travel when and where you want, but also the full responsibility to pay for the vehicle and its upkeep.

To represent the range and flexibility of MVaaS, three approaches are used: a taxi, rental car and leased car. The first MVaaS example is similar to using a taxi where you get in someone else's vehicle and he or she takes you where you direct. The owner of the taxi maintains full responsibility for the operation and upkeep. In the rental car example you drive it and gas it (For the sake of comparison, video production services remain under your responsibility). Again, the owner has responsibility for the upkeep. The final example is to lease a car where someone else owns it, but you drive it, provide gas and own some responsibility for the operation and upkeep.

The following diagram is for illustration purposes only and not intended to be representative of all MVaaS approaches. Self-managed is inclusive of staffing with internal resources.

---

[34] Doug Bannister, Founder and CEO of Omnivex

Digital Touch Points

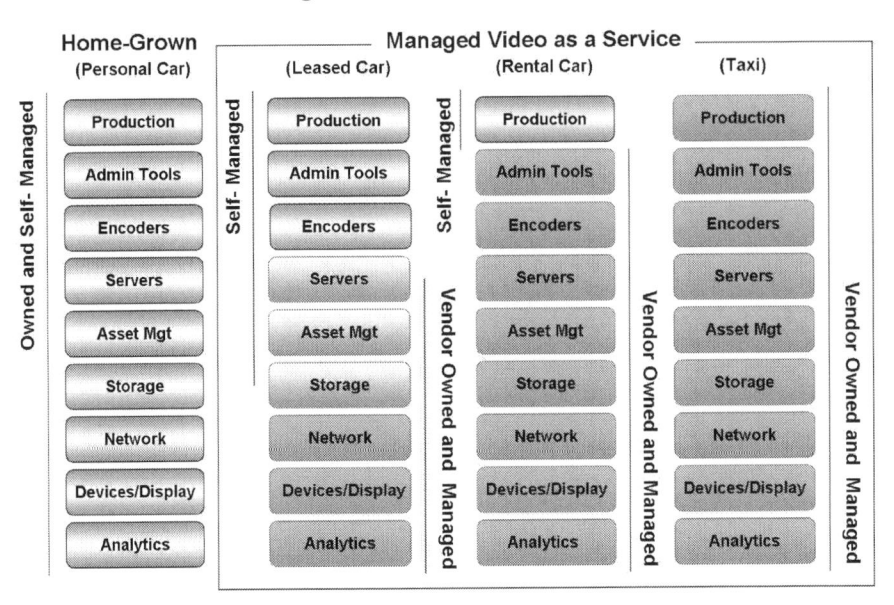

Home-grown and MVaaS Options

Home-Grown	Managed Video as a Service		
(Personal Car)	(Leased Car)	(Rental Car)	(Taxi)

Owned and Self-Managed | Self-Managed | Vendor Owned and Managed | Vendor Owned and Managed | Vendor Owned and Managed

Categories (shown for each column): Production, Admin Tools, Encoders, Servers, Asset Mgt, Storage, Network, Devices/Display, Analytics

Managed Staffing Resources as a Service

Managed service is not only about equipment and systems. A growing aspect of MVaaS is staffing services which as depicted in the examples can be packaged with the acquisition of equipment and systems or function as a stand-alone service.

The World Bank Group (Bank) – The Bank hosts thousands of on-premise meetings at its headquarters in Washington, D.C. each year. It has about two-hundred meeting and conference rooms which are supported by an extensive range of audiovisual, video production, webcast and videoconference capabilities. In addition, the Bank has an extensive digital signage network and video display systems to support both institutional and departmental spaces.

While the Bank owns and maintains all equipment and systems, it outsources the staffing through MVaaS to operate and maintain them as well as design and integrate new systems and capabilities. The number of staff is significant and increases as the size and scope of the Bank's audiovisual operation continues to expand.

International Monetary Fund – The International Monetary Fund (IMF) is closely aligned with the Bank, serving many of the same international member countries. Also headquartered in Washington, D.C., the IMF has video capabilities and requirements similar to the Bank's.

The IMF also outsources its staffing services through MvaaS to operate, maintain and implement IMF owned equipment.

In addition to system operation, call center and help desk support, and maintenance, a key element to staffing is providing customer service. This may include: providing creative services, input to business strategies, client education and training, operation of the systems, and tracking of industry trends, innovative applications, new media and best practices.

Role of the Vendor

Another improving aspect of video in the enterprise is the role of industry vendors. In an effort to maintain a competitive advantage, some vendors have expanded their business opportunities by offering their products and services as MVaaS. This includes integrators of video production and audiovisual systems, providers of two-way videoconference and telepresence systems and satellite-based business television and interactive distance learning systems. Also, they are partnering with or acquiring other businesses to expand their over-all offerings.

Best-of-breed companies are looking to contracted vendors to see if they are providing MVaaS and expanding their offerings to address more aspects of the video ecosystem. Successful companies should find a vendor who can perform as a trusted advisor as well as provider of a wide range of systems and services.

Although, MVaaS is gaining traction, keep in mind that it may not be the right approach for your company or it may not be the right time. Some companies are very comfortable with the home-grown and self-managed approach and/or they find great value in purchasing systems and services from different vendors. Also, some companies may be in the early-to-mid stages of system implementations and a change to this business approach may be too disruptive to the operation.

Service Level Agreements & Key Performance Indicators

Service level agreements (SLA) are a standard business practice for most equipment and service contracts. The primary function of the SLA is to set mutually agreed upon expectations with the vendor to measure performance. Typical SLA benchmarks may include implementation timelines, equipment failure rates, quality levels, help desk and support response times and system restoration time frames.

Whereas, SLAs are forward-looking, key performance indicators (KPIs) are used to measure performance of a vendor as established in the SLA. In addition to the KPIs related to the media business strategy, KPI coverage for equipment and services may include:

- Equipment:
    - Availability;
    - Out-of-box failures;
- System implementations:
    - Research and design timeframe;
    - Number of systems integrated;
    - System certified and put in use;
- Operational support services:
    - Number of programs or events;
    - Number experiencing incidents;
    - Help desk(s) response;
    - Support availability;
        - Number resolved;
- Technical support services:
    - Mean time between failures;
    - Mean time to repair;

- o Mean time to system restoration;
- o Dollars spent;
- ➤ On-site staffing services;
  - o In-room response;
  - o Help desk response;
  - o Mean time between failures;
  - o Mean time to repair;
  - o Mean time to system restoration;
  - o Dollars spent;
  - o Customer service and satisfaction;
  - o Operational improvements;
  - o Staffing and service strategies.

The list of KPIs can be extensive, with many of them applicable to multiple areas. However, they should be relevant to each specific vendor agreement and include appropriate conditions, penalties and incentives (where applicable).

The use of both SLAs and KPIs is necessary as the technology has become more complex and services more involved. They should be included in every agreement for video and dynamic media equipment and services regardless of the purchasing approach, e.g.: MVaaS or home-grown.

Business Drivers and Key Benefits

Business Drivers may include:

- ➤ Managed Costs – No up-front costs, with predictable, fixed monthly costs.
- ➤ Mitigated Risk – Avoid exposure to equipment or software obsolescence as vendor owns responsibility.
- ➤ Contracted services – Outsource staffing services to better manage head count and labor costs.
- ➤ Specialized Expertise – Leverage vendor's access to talent pools.
- ➤ Future-proof System and Operation – Leverage vendor's knowledge of, and industry research

regarding, new media and technologies, applications, and industry best practices.

Benefits may include:

- Improved Quality and System Performance - Vendor will provide system refresh or upgrades to improve or meet performance standards and/or to improve operational efficiencies and reduce costs.
- Business Continuity – Future purchases and enhancements can be achieved through an existing contract vehicle with less disruption to operations.
- Improved Communications - Focus on core business (increasing and digital touch points and improving the bottom-line) while vendor handles day-to-day communications, production and system challenges.
- Sustained Operational Expertise - Vendor can be a resource for fresh creative talent and skilled operators.
- Sustained Budget – Manage system and operation within forecast budget and financial plan.

Tips and Recommendations

- Identify the acquisition, maintenance and staffing method best suited to your company's business approach: Home-grown, MVaaS or combination.
- Evaluate the existing systems and operation to determine which ones could apply to MVaaS if not the entire video ecosystem.
- Migrate to MVaaS as part of a well-thought-out business strategy and implementation plan.
- Identify a vendor(s) to engage as a trusted advisor as well as provider of systems and services.
- Leverage the resources and industry knowledge of the MVaaS provider to:

Manage and enhance the company's video and dynamic media capabilities;

Stay current with industry trends and new media innovation;

Manage staffing resources and keep current with required skills;

Manage capital expenditures and maintain fixed costs;

Mitigate risks associated with equipment and system obsolescence.

Digital Touch Points

Summary

Roadmap to Success

Use the information (perspectives, recommendations and tips) in this book to utilize video and dynamic media to increase the touch points with your customers and employees. Improve the quality of their experience and your company is likely to gain a competitive advantage and see a positive impact on business goals.

Start by developing a comprehensive media business strategy that is inclusive of all business groups and stakeholders. A collaborative effort will result in a clear understanding of each group's needs and objectives. It will help identify the company's existing systems, the reach of their capabilities and what your company does know about internal and external media channels. More important, it will provide the foundation to find out what your company does not know about available technology and capabilities.

The next step is to conduct a thorough analysis to identify the business, operational and technical requirements relevant to the mutual needs of the business groups and incorporate them into the company's business and communication implementation plans.

Save time, resources and money by engaging the services of an industry specialist to:

    Provide industry knowledge and perspective;
    Conduct a Gap Analysis of systems, capabilities and resources;
    Provide structure, processes and guidance.

Digital Touch Points

Resources

Introduction

Steve Ballmer, Microsoft CEO (USA Today, January 2011).

Palubiak, Randy, *Digital Touch Points: Reaching your audience on all four screens*, Hughes Network Systems (2012).

Executive Overview

Manning, Harley and Bodine, Kerry. *Outside In: The Power of Putting Customers at the Center of Your Business*, Amazon (2012).

Video as a Strategic Communications Tool

The Kennedy / Nixon Debates (History.com).

Nixon, Richard M., *Six Crises*, Doubleday (1962).

Matthew Fraser and Soumitra Dutta (2008), *Barack Obama and the Facebook Election USNews* (November 2008).

Dr. Pamela Rutledge, *How Obama Won the Social Media Battle in 2012 Presidential Campaign* (Media Psychology, January 2013).

Cisco Live Conference (July 2011).

Nielsen, *Internet and Mobile Video Audiences* (May 2012) Marketingcharts.com

Matt Pillar, *Capture Online Sales with Digital Signage*, Integrated Solutions for Retailers (February 2013).

U.S. Online Video Use Up 45 Percent, Year-Over-Year (2011) Clickz.com

Digital Touch Points - Reach and Empower Customers and Employees

What is Digital Place-based Media? Dp-aa.org

Content is King

Peter Bloniarz, Dean of the College of Computing and Information at the University of Albany, State University of New York, *Atlanta Journal Constitution* (December 2008).

Berge, T. (1990). *The First 24-Hours,* Cambridge, MA: Basil Blackwell, Inc. (1990).

Rollins Corporation Takes Learning Global, (December 2012) Globecommsystems.com

Dr. Jolly Holden, and Dr. Philip Westfall, *An Instructional Media Selection Guide for Distance Learning - Implications for Blended Learning* (2010) USDLA.org

Digital Touch Points

Establish a Media Business Strategy

Viewing Locations and Environments

Blend Enterprise-wide Digital Media Channels

Dr. Philip Westfall, *The Government Education & Training Network (GETN): making HDTV and IPTV cost-effective options for distance learning.* Presentation at Society for Applied Learning Technology (SALT) Conference (August 2013).

Paul R. La Monica, Doritos: You create our Super Bowl commercial, CNNMoney.com (September 2006).

Dan L., A brief history of the Crash the Super Bowl contest, VideoContestNews.com (January 2012).

Doritos Crashes the Superbowl, IPRA Press Release 2007

Lisa Arthur, *Three Lessons from Pepsi's Super Bowl XLV Ad Campaign* Forbes.com (February 2011).

E.J. Schultz, *Why 'Crash the Super Bowl' Hasn't Burned Out for Doritos* Adage.com (January 2013).

A Medical Leader Brings New Innovations to Patient Care with Apps for iPhone, iPad, and iPad Mini' (2013), Apple.com (2013).

Chris Murphy, From Lowe's to Coke, 8 CEOs Talk Tech Strategy (April 9, 2012) InformationWeek (2012)

Webopedia.com

Gerben Meijer, *"The Cloud" vs The Internet* cloudproviderusa.com (October 2012).

Analytics

Preserve and Protect Media Assets

USA Today (July 2011), analysis by Standard & Poor's Capital IQ.

What is a Digital Asset Management System (DAM)? Contentmanager.eu.com

Dublin Core Metadata Element Set (DCMES), Dublincore.org

Mayoclinic.com

Us.coca-cola.com

Managed Video as a Service

Bob Dylan, The Times They Are A-Changin' (1964).

Doug Bannister, Founder and CEO of Omnivex

About the Author

Randy Palubiak is the president and founding partner of Enliten Management Group, Inc., a media business consulting firm. He is an industry analyst and media business strategist with over 35 years of experience in visual communications covering broadcast television, media and video production and enterprise communications.

Randy helps companies create their media business strategies and select the video and dynamic-media solutions and vendors to provide the most effective blend of media channels to meet their business requirements.

Randy is on the Board of Directors and an advisor to numerous associations and organizations. He is the recipient of industry awards for producing and directing commercials, corporate videos and image campaigns. He is a recognized speaker and presenter, has written numerous publications, white papers, and proprietary reports and has co-authored two industry books: *Delivery of Media in the Enterprise* and *The BTV/IP Receiver Guide*.

Digital Touch Points

Enliten Management Group, Inc.

enliten.net